Racing in the time of the Super-Teams

A REVIEW OF THE
2021 ROAD RACING SEASON

YOUCAXTON
PUBLICATIONS

ISBN 978-1-914424-34-2

Published by YouCaxton Publications 2021

Contents

PLATES

1. June 29, Fougères: Mark Cavendish wins his first Tour de France stage since 2016. The Manxman would go on to take a further three stages, equalling Eddy Merckx's record of 34 career Tour stage wins. *Alex Broadway/SWpix.com*
2. July 7, Mont Ventoux: Tadej Pogačar descends the bald mountain in pursuit of Jonas Vingegaard en route to the finish at Malaucène. Eleven days later the Slovenian would seal his second Tour win in two years. *Alex Broadway/SWpix.com*
3. July 25, Fuji Speedway: Anna Kiesenhofer recovers after taking gold in the women's Olympic road race. The Austrian broke away at the start and rode the final phase solo to win by 1min15sec from Annemiek van Vleuten. *Alex Whitehead/SWpix.com*
4. October 9, Felixstowe: Demi Vollering celebrates victory in the AJ Bell Tour of Britain. *Simon Wilkinson/SWpix.com*
5. September 2, Fuji Speedway: gold medallist Sarah Storey leads her GB team mate Crystal Lane-Wright in the C4-5 road race; Storey took her career medal total to 28 at Tokyo 2021, making her the most successful British Paralympian ever. *Alex Whitehead/SWpix.com*
6. September 11, Edinburgh: Pascal Eeenkorn hands a bottle to 12-year-old Xander Graham as the winning break approaches the finish of stage seven of the Tour of Britain. Yves Lampaert went on to win the stage. *Alex Whitehead/SWpix.com*
7. September 26, Leuven: Julian Alaphilippe makes his winning attack on Sint Antoniusberg with 17 kilometres remaining to the finish of the men's world road race championship; behind, Sonny Colbrelli and Neilson Powless are unable to respond. *Alex Broadway/SWpix.com*
8. September, Flanders: as well as Leuven, Antwerp, Knokke-Heist and Bruges were among the venues at the world road race championships, the first time Belgium had hosted the event since Zolder in 2002. *Alex Broadway/SWpix.com*
9. October 2, Roubaix: Lizzie Deignan catches her breath after making history as the first winner of Paris-Roubaix Femmes. She finished 1min 17sec ahead of Marianne Vos. *Tim van Wichelen/Cor Vos/SWpix.com*

For more cycling images go to www.swpix.com

Foreword

As we learned to live with the Pandemic, 2021 was the year when cycling returned to "normal". A new normal, one where riders and team staff wore masks as routine, where PCR tests were just another bit of pre-race protocol, and where the media were banned from the start area at major races because the Covid-19 pandemic had provided the perfect excuse for doing so.

At *lacourseentete.com* there was a "new normal" as well. From being a fun venture to launch while normal life was suspended, the website became a fun part of the furniture for writers, podcasters and designers. There were kind reviews of the "pop-up" year book that we launched in November 2020 – two days after the Vuelta ended – to test the waters. Our partnership with *Peloton* magazine continued and deepened, and so we got up and did it all over again. Which as anyone involved with sport knows, is always the hard part.

Here at the website, some things haven't changed. We've continued in our mission to find new writers, to write stuff that appeals to us as writers, and to report the sport in different ways, striving to push for the agendas we feel matter. We still don't aim slavishly to cover everything blow by blow, aiming instead to provide perspective and fine writing, driven by writers not editors. We want to have fun, and with any luck the pages that follow will convey the passion we feel for this sport, and the excitement it manages to transmit to us after – in some cases – frankly too many years to figure out.

So welcome to our second review of the year. Just like the first, it doesn't try to offer a comprehensive take on everything that took place. It boils down to what interested each of our writers on a given day in a given way. This was an intense year's racing, with more of the fresh energy we'd seen in 2021 following through after cycling's shortest ever winter. This was the year of Mark Cavendish's incredible comeback, Anna van der Breggen's retirement after one of the finest careers on record, Wout van Aert's emergence as the consummate all rounder, Anna Kiesenhofer's triumph over the Orange machine, tears of joy from Mathieu van der Poel and Ellen van Dijk, and massive surprises from Elena Balsamo and Julian Alaphilippe. And much much more.

Enjoy the ride.

The *lacourseentete.com* team.

Introduction: Racing in the Time of the Super-Teams

By William Fotheringham, October 1 2021

It's funny to think that there was a time not long ago when the big question in men's cycling was this: how on earth do you beat Team Sky? And it's salutary to remember that there is one team which, right now, is probably more dominant and star-studded than any squad ever has been in cycling: the Dutch women's national team, whose dominance of its chosen domain – the road world championships – is unprecedented.

What do these two things have to do with each other, you might well ask? The answer is this: they are two aspects of the same phenomenon, the rise in cycling in the 21st century of the "super-team", with reach and power – be it financial or simply tactical – that give them pre-eminence in their particular field, and make it increasingly hard for the opposition to cope.

The statistics are explicit. In men's cycling, you can name four "super-teams": Ineos, Jumbo-Visma, UAE and Deceuninck-Quickstep. The last rider from a team other than the first three to win a Grand Tour was Richard Carapaz at the Giro in 2019. As for DQS, as is widely known, they mop up most of the rest: by the end of September 2021, they were north of 60 wins. That's on a par with 2019 (62) and 2018 (74). Looking at the Grand Tours in 2021, 12 of the 21 stages in the Tour de France went to the Big Four, at the Vuelta it was 10 of the 21. That might not sound so bad, until you recall there are 19 other teams in each Grand Tour.

Let's turn to the Orange Train. Between 2017 and 2020 they swept the board at the world road race championship with

Chantal Blaak (2017), Annemiek van Vleuten (2019) and Anna van der Breggen (2018, 2020). At the time trial world championship it was a similar picture, with only Chloe Dygart (2019) breaking the monopoly – van Vleuten, 2017, 2018, van der Breggen (2020) and Ellen van Dijk (2021). Of the 15 medals available in those five years, the Dutch took 11. At the European road race championships, there's been one non-Dutch win in the last five years. Yes, this year in Leuven the machine derailed, but it was an exceptional event.

The rise of the Super-Teams has taken place in different ways, because men's and women's cycling are at contrasting phases of development. The rise of the Dutch women is historic, a classic case of a nation that invested early and has reaped the rewards. In the early 1970s it already looked as if Holland had a more enlightened attitude to women racing bikes; the rise of Léontien van Moorsel and Marianne Vos seems like an extension of that, and as role models they have inspired a constant emergence of talented women in recent years. Talented individuals will usually break through, but in national terms, success clearly breeds success. Vos, van der Breggen and van Vleuten are the figureheads of a golden generation, but national teams being what they are, it may be that in a few years the wheel will turn again, and Dutch dominance will be a thing of the past.

Men's professional cycling is different, because here the super teams depend on the cheque book. Since the arrival of Team Sky in men's cycling in 2010, the sport has gone through an initial phase of trying to figure out what the hell had hit it, and it's now in a second phase where teams have figured out that if you can't beat them, you join them, and if you can't join them, you can't beat them.

The Team Sky philosophy was pretty overt from the moment that Bradley Wiggins was induced to break his contract with Garmin at the end of 2009: the money will do most of the heavy lifting. So Team Sky began by hiring middle ranking riders who might have been border-line leadership material in other squads, and turning them into super-domestiques: Michael Rogers, Christian Knees, Edvald Boasson-Hagen, Peter Kennaugh, Geraint Thomas. Over the years, the riders they could muster grew better and the budget grew in proportion. There were world champions – Michał Kwiatkowski – and Grand Tour winners such as Carapaz. That brought us to the point where, as Team Ineos in 2021, they were fielding teams with three Grand Tour winners at the Tour de France – Carapaz, Thomas and Tao Geogheghan Hart – and two at the Vuelta, with Carapaz and Egan Bernal. And they are still recruiting podium contenders as domestiques: Richie Porte, Dani Martínez, Pavel Sivakov.

For other teams, you match that in one or both of two ways: you buy big or you buy clever. UAE and Jumbo have done a bit of both, in hiring, respectively, Tadej Pogačar and Wout van Aert – and it's worth recalling that in recruiting the Belgian from Verandahs Willems in 2018, there was an element of the Team Sky vs Garmin battle over Wiggins. At the end of 2021, UAE's recruitment in particular made it clear how they were going to take on Ineos: they've bought in João Almeida, Pascal Ackermann, George Bennett, Marc Soler as well as two of the best youngsters out there in Finn Fisher-Black and Juan Ayuso. *Procycling* magazine recently described this as the PSG-ification of cycling, and the soccer paralells are instructive, with the increasing concentration of talent and budget at a few teams. If UAE are PSG, does that make Ineos the equivalent of Real Madrid with their host of *Galácticos*, and Jumbo Manchester United?

Deceuninck would probably be Arsenal, boxing clever off a lower budget, not winning the very biggest trophies, but punching well above their weight through intelligent and ruthless management. Until Remco Evenepoel reaches his full potential, they won't be pushing to win the Grand Tours, but will remain based on what works: an outstanding sprint train onto which you can bolt any fastman in the peloton, and a core of clever and well directed Classics riders.

Cycling has had super-teams before, but not on this scale. In 1979-80, the TI-Raleigh squad were dominant although they won only one Tour de France, and in the mid-1980s, it was La Vie Claire with Bernard Hinault and Greg LeMond. But the difference now, in men's cycling, is that the biggest teams are built to last longer and are expected to dominate on every front. Raleigh weren't successful across the board; La Vie Claire were at their peak only in 1985 and 1986. Ineos and the others seem to be in it for the long haul.

Outside the world and European championships, where the Dutch dominate, women's cycling is in a different phase, because its team budgets are such that the most talented riders are already spread more widely outside the two dominant teams, SD Worx and Trek-Segafredo, and that's likely to continue. The rapid expansion of the women's stage race calendar, in the wake of the inception – at long last – of the Tour de France Femmes, will see a parallel expansion in teams similar to what happened in men's cycling when the Tour de France went global in the mid-1980s. There's likely to be a further dispersal of the best riders initially as an increased number of teams look to snap up the most talented women.

Can anything be done to curb the rise of the super-teams, and should it? In sport, it's hard to manipulate the market. You can talk about salary caps, but there are always ways around them. But we are perfectly entitled to feel uneasy about the lavishing of cash and resources on what is, in essence, something pretty damn frivolous. It's also reasonable to feel queasy at the inequalities within the sport. I will never forget a conversation with Lizzie Deignan where we speculated on the cost of a women's WorldTour team and estimated it at roughly one Spanish super-domestique. Male, obviously.

The answer, perhaps, is for governing bodies to try and force the big teams to channel some of that cash elsewhere. The most enlightened teams are already running men's and women's WorldTour teams in parallel, and that trend will continue without compulsion, because it makes such obvious good sense in PR and publicity terms. There's an equally clear case for taking a levy off the biggest budgets and directing it at rider development, and for rewarding teams that invest in under-23 and junior squads. But you can't reverse history. The super-teams are here to stay.

What does the emergence of the super-teams mean for cycling fans? Generally, it's all to the good, because of the narratives it creates. At the Olympic Games this summer, Anna Kiesenhofer's victory in the women's road race made for suspense, intrigue and prestige, because it came at the expense of arguably the strongest national team ever fielded: van Vleuten, van der Breggen, Demi Vollering and Marianne Vos. Something similar happened in the European championship in Glasgow in 2018, when Marta Bastianelli broke the Dutch dominance; in Leuven, the plot line was obvious: can anyone beat the Dutch? Well, Balsamo could. You can't deny the fascination in watching Ineos, UAE and Jumbo knock chunks out of each other in the Tour and Vuelta in 2021. Peter Cossins argues later in this compilation that the men's side of the sport is going through a golden age at present, and that's partly down to the fact that the Tour de France is no longer a simple matter of Sir Dave Brailsford fielding eight high-value men and one of them winning.

There's an interest as well in how the other teams react; paradoxically, in men's cycling, the Super-Teams haven't made for more structured, contained racing, partly because the other teams know they have to scrap for every crumb. Squads such as

EF Education and DSM (and, at the Giro this year, Qhubeka-Assos) have become more inventive in how they approach stage wins at the Grand Tours because they know the upper reaches of the overall standings are increasingly difficult to attain.

The result of that is the fantastic racing so many stages of the Grand Tours now produce, light years from the formulaic stuff we saw in the time of Miguel Indurain and Lance Armstrong. I've already mentioned the lustre the Orange armada have brought to the major women's championships, and parallel with that, the question of how Lizzie Deignan, Elisa Longo-Borghini, Vos and van Vleuten will take on the SDWorx steamroller has brought a fresh frisson to every Women's WorldTour Classic from Binda to Plouay. With any luck, we'll see that story line in 2022 in the Tour de France Femmes as well.

Chapter One: Trailblazers, a Nearly Man and VDB nears the End

CAV AND PAT: PUTTING THE BAND BACK ON THE ROAD

By William Fotheringham, December 14 2020

Back in April 2018, I was invited to a bit of a get-together in deepest Flanders to celebrate the 20th anniversary of Quickstep Floors' sponsorship of Patrick Lefevere's team, today known as Deceuninck-Quickstep. There were various luminaries from the team's sponsors, a smattering of bike riders, and greats from past incarnations of the squad, most notably Johan Museeuw, Paolo Bettini and Oscar Freire, but not, surprisingly, the best of them all: Tom Boonen.

Another surprise was to bump into Mark Cavendish, who had taken the trouble to nip over from Dimension Data's team hotel. If my memory serves me right, Cavendish was the only active rider there who wasn't riding for Quickstep. And the Manxman didn't just pop in, press the flesh and beetle off back to his hotel. Boonen's absence made Cavendish's presence there just that little bit more significant; when you're a team owner celebrating a sponsor's longevity, you want your former world champions to be in the room to help you do it.

I wouldn't say that Cavendish's presence that evening explains Lefevere's decision to hire him for 2021, a decision announced a few weeks ago to a rash of raised eyebrows across the piece. Of course it doesn't. But it does illustrate that the links between the best sprinter of all time and the winningest team in cycling run pretty deep, and that does go some way to making Cav's return to the Belgian squad easier to understand.

Lefevere isn't the kind who will just ask "how high?" when a former rider asks him to jump. The Flemish manager has been in the game since the early 80s, and he knows that professional cycling is a "what have you done for me lately?" kind of sport. He himself has a personal rule, according to the writer Philippe le Gars of *l'Equipe*, that if you leave the DQS or OPQS fold, you don't come back in. His thinking, apparently, is that if a rider chooses another team, that means there is no reason for him to return. He's made an exception for only a few riders; Cavendish, is, apparently, the only example of a non-Flemish rider who has been offered a second chance with Lefevere.

It's easy to forget that Cavendish enjoyed the second most successful season of his entire career with Lefevere and company. For most of us, the default is that Cavendish was in his prime in the long-distant High Road years. In 2013 at Omega-Pharma-Quickstep he won 19 races, including his 100th career victory at the Giro, where he was on stunning form, with five stage wins, and the points prize which meant he had been crowned best sprinter at all three Grand Tours. He took the British national title in Glasgow, and at the Tour de France, OPQS engineered him a stunning victory in the crosswinds on stage 13 into Saint-Amand-Montrond.

No one expects Cavendish to repeat his achievements of 2013 in 2021, although it's amusing to remember that seven years ago at the Tour de France, questions were already being asked about his future as a sprinter because Marcel Kittel was on such unbeatable form. But the reference to the here and now is this: team managers remember those great moments; they create an emotional bond.

That's why, when Lefevere saw Cavendish getting in the break in several of the Belgian Classics last year – a completely atypical thing for the Manxman to do – and took his phone call, he didn't dismiss out of hand the idea of Cav finishing his career with him. Yes, Cavendish may struggle to find his place in the team at times, given the wealth of hungry young talent in there, but the reality is that cycling has moved on in the four years since he was in his pomp, and that would apply wherever he went.

No one knows what Cavendish will achieve in 2021. Many followers of the sport feel he's finished, and some seem to take a positive pleasure in his struggles. But three things are certain. The 2020 season can't have worked in his favour. There was uncertainty at Bahrain-McLaren, and uncertainty for much of the season. Once racing got going again, there were relatively few chances for any sprinters. Older riders didn't seem to find form as easily as the younger generation. There was no opportunity for anyone to ride into form: it either happened or it didn't. If 2021 is closer to the pattern of a "normal" season, that will help his cause.

The second certainty is that if any rider gets back into a positive spiral of form and success, surprising things can happen, and there is probably a better chance of that scenario happening for Cavendish at a well-structured team like DQS than in most places.

The final point is this: most of the greats struggle to make a perfectly neat end to their careers, because the qualities which make them great militate against just walking away. Ask Greg LeMond, Eddy Merckx, or even Sean Kelly. If Cavendish and Lefevere can engineer anything close to a neat conclusion, they will have done better than most.

LAEVENS' COMING OUT SHOWS CYCLING'S LACK OF LGBTQ+ REPRESENTATION

By Sadhbh O'Shea, January 11 2021

The Black Lives Matter protests that followed the death of George Floyd in the summer of 2020 forced society to confront racism in dramatic fashion. The sense of feeling that grew out of that moment was so strong that even cycling, which is not known for being in any way progressive, had to acknowledge it – though the response was pretty lacklustre.

Sport as a whole has historically been particularly good at ignoring social concerns and poor at reflecting society, although wider issues can sometimes breach the bubble sport has created for itself, such as Colin Kaepernick taking the knee or Emily Wilding Davison stepping in front of King George's horse at the 1913 Derby.

People say that sport and politics shouldn't be mixed but sport isn't and shouldn't be a comfort blanket for bigots, racists and sexists. Largely the domain of the straight white male, sport has gradually changed its ways over the years but there is still a long way to travel on a number of major issues.

Cycling has further to go on dealing with social inequalities than most sports. You just need to look at how difficult it has been to engage the sport in providing any sort of parity for women, then wonder how long it will be before any efforts are made to drive towards racial equality.

Racism and gender inequality are by far not the only issues cycling has to tackle. Last week a u23 cyclo-cross rider by the name of Justin Laevens came out as gay. He might not be a household name in the sport but this is an important moment for the sport. When the news hit the English-speaking press, I saw many comments saying "who cares?" or "why is this news?". It should not be news, but it is. These comments miss the point about just how hard it can be for an athlete to come out and how important it can be for other LGBTQ+ people to see it happen. Sport can create a narrow idea of what a man, a woman and an athlete should be and it can be intimidating to identify yourself as being outside this prescribed "norm". Representation, as it is with all demographics of society, is hugely important.

In a world where same-sex couples can marry and there is increasing awareness of the transgender community, frighteningly few male cyclists have come out as LGBTQ+ while actively racing. Those that do come out are often retired from the sport by the time they feel safe and comfortable to do so.

Figures by the UK's office for national statistics show that about 2.2% of the population identify as being gay, lesbian or bisexual. In women's cycling, it is not unusual to meet openly lesbian or bisexual riders or team staff members. However, to the best of my knowledge, there are no openly gay or bisexual riders in the top tiers of the men's side of the sport.

With nearly 1,000 riders at WorldTour and ProTeam level, the chances of there being not one LGBTQ+ rider among them is far-fetched. Being homosexual or heterosexual doesn't make you more or less likely to be interested in sport. However, the idea that you might not be welcome or that you may have to hide who you are is likely to turn some away or force them into hiding their identity. Life as a professional athlete is difficult enough without the feeling that you must hide who you are to your teammates and the rest of the world.

The old-school boys club culture that still runs through professional cycling isn't overly welcoming to those that fit outside certain prescribed stereotypes. As sure as I am that there are LGBTQ+ riders within the men's peloton, I am sure that there are those who would be incredibly welcoming to any teammate that came out. However, there will also be those who would be vocally against it, and those who, while they wouldn't object to a gay teammate, would make uneducated remarks and jokes. It only takes a small group of people like this to make a person's life difficult.

I wish Justin Laevens well in his career and I hope that his example can help others feel as if they don't have to hide themselves and encourage them to feel brave enough come out, whatever their orientation. However, they shouldn't have to feel brave to be true to themselves. Cycling needs to rid itself of its old-school mentality and actively make an effort to ensure the sport is a more welcoming place.

"I FEEL READY": TRAILBLAZER CHERIE PRIDHAM BECOMES A WORLDTOUR DS

By Nick Bull, Februrary 9 2021

There's a moment from Israel Start-Up Nation's training camp in Spain at the start of the year that stands out for Cherie Pridham. "I was sitting next to a rider and we were just chatting about normal things, nothing cycling related, on the team bus heading back to the airport," she said. "Then all of a sudden they said 'you're just like one of the other DSs!'."

A fair and accurate comment, yes, but it is worth remembering that Pridham is anything but. As the manager then owner of Team Raleigh and Vitus Pro Cycling, two UK-based UCI Continental squads that ran from 2011 through to 2020, she was already a trailblazer. Shortly after the pandemic forced her team to close at the end of last year, she became the first female *directeur sportif* at WorldTour level after joining Israel Start-Up Nation. *The New York Times*, little known for its cycling reportage, covered her appointment. The response to being unveiled on 4 December has, in her own words, only just begun to quieten.

She said: "I genuinely assumed there would be a bit of hoo-ha and that there'd be some criticism because I'm a woman before things moved on. Yet a couple of weeks later I was still doing interviews with media all around the world. The number of private messages I had from women of all ages was incredible. I didn't expect that. A few weeks later it dawned on me that perhaps I do have a responsibility to those people here, and I can help them out by sharing my experiences and proving that by being an optimistic person it's possible to grab those opportunities."

Pridham's path to the WorldTour began when she started racing aged 11. Born in the UK but raised in South Africa (owing to her father's job in the Royal Navy), she rode eight Tours

Cycliste Féminin and the Giro Rosa twice during a lengthy pro career that included spells on Belgian, French, Italian and Swiss teams. "I think I'm a fighter," she said, attributing that to her experiences as a teenager and young adult. "I had to find my feet when I came back to the UK, pretty much without my family, and my racing career came before women's teams started to become more professional."

Spells managing junior teams and British domestic squads post-retirement led to her teaming up with Raleigh as they relaunched a men's team 10 years ago. She purchased the team in late 2013. "Even at this time I never gave the idea that I might be a trailblazer," she added. "Cycling is just a way of life for me. I just crack on."

The decision to close Vitus down first entered her mind last autumn. Like all British Continental teams, the relentless battle to secure funding played a key role in Pridham's decision, combined with the uncertainty of a domestic racing calendar featuring few high-profile events and even fewer that are insulated from the effects of Covid-19.

She said: "It felt like the right time for me. I couldn't do it half-hearted. For example, I've always cared about how the team looked – historically I think that we've looked bigger than we actually were based on our appearance – and I wouldn't have wanted that to change. I look back and think 'I've done that now'. We had such good times between 2011 and 2016. Budgets were a bit more fruitful off the back of London 2012. We weren't just racing in the UK – we were going all over the place. In the moment we probably didn't realise how fortunate we were. It was during this time that I made the decision to start looking at what I could do next. During that process I asked myself 'why can't I send emails to WorldTour teams?'."

Incredibly, barely a couple of hours after the decision to close Vitus was made final on a mid-November evening, Israel's general manager Kjell Carlström approached Pridham about joining the fledgling team. "All credit to Kjell – from my first conversation with him he wasn't as interested in my CV as he was exploring how I could fit into the team and what Israel Start-Up Nation can do to become more diverse," she said. "The team's approach is really refreshing. No one rider is bigger than the team."

Pridham said she attended the team's pre-Christmas DS camp in Girona, at which the 2021 race programme was mapped out, with a "massive smile" on her face. Not even a week of 11-hour days detracted from the enjoyment of her new surroundings. As detailed plans for this year (complete with lengthy pandemic-related contingency) emerged, the extent of the step up from Continental level (where UK teams operating with a yearly budget of £250,000 are increasingly rare) to the multi-million pound nature of the WorldTour became clear.

"Budget is clearly the most significant thing, absolutely no stone is left unturned," she said. "There's a really good structure here. The team have brought in [Grand Tour stage winner] Rik Verbrugghe as our head DS and signing riders like Chris [Froome], Sep [Vanmarcke] and Michael [Woods] shows how we're trying to grow. We're still a very young team and are the underdogs of the WorldTour. There are so many other talented people behind the scenes; going from trying to oversee the commercial, business and sporting jobs singlehandedly at a Continental team to this has taken a bit of getting used to. I'm learning every day."

And what of the step up to WorldTour level and the new races that she'll encounter in 2021? "I try not to get too drawn into the fact that they're WorldTour races. The concept of preparation doesn't change; I get to use VeloViewer on a daily basis now. I've never had that opportunity before. I can look online and watch old footage. There are websites full of information and results. I think the big thing for me is getting a feel about the flow of these races. Even then, looking at how racing has been since last summer, it feels like it has changed. There's a new dynamic to it – I think it has become more aggressive. There are more challenges for teams. They need to think even more about how they use their riders now."

Covid depending, Pridham will make her debut in the team car in the coming month – nearly a year on from Vitus' last international hurrah at Le Samyn, which coincidentally was won by Israel's Hugo Hofstetter last March. She admits that the significance of the occasion is not lost on her. "I'm no dummy, I know people's eyes will be on me for the first races," Pridham said. "But I feel ready to hit the ground running now."

TAO TAKES A STAND WHILE TAKING THE KNEE

By Nick Bull, February 19 2021

Arguably the most unedifying moment of "The Last Dance", the acclaimed 2020 ESPN and Netflix documentary revolving around Michael Jordan, is when the basketball star talks about a Senate race in North Carolina some 30 years earlier. Explaining his reasons for not publicly supporting Democrat challenger Harvey Gantt against Republican incumbent Jesse Helms, the six-time NBA champion (who was raised in the state) noted that "Republicans buy sneakers, too".

Jordan, who has made over $1 billion from his partnership with Nike, the manufacturer of his Air Jordan shoes, claimed the comment was made in jest. Explaining his position, he added: "The way I go about my life is I set examples. If it inspires you? Great, I will continue to do that. If it doesn't? Then maybe I'm not the person you should be following." Among those talking heads in the documentary who discussed the issue was Barack Obama, who admitted that he "would've wanted to see Michael push harder" against Helms. "On the other hand," the 44th President said "he was still trying to figure out, 'How am I managing this image that has been created around me, and how do I live up to it?'"

Judging by the way Tao Geoghegan Hart spoke out so impressively against cycling's diversity and inclusivity problem on Thursday, the 25-year-old Giro d'Italia winner seemingly already knows how to manage the image around him – the thinking man's Bradley Wiggins, if you like – *and* what he can do to meet expectations.

Geogheghan Hart's advocacy should be of little surprise to cycling fans. He has long been a cheerleader for women's cycling. Anybody who read his blogs dating back nearly a decade would have got a feel for how mature and considered the Londoner is. His self-effacing comments yesterday – "I have not done enough" – shows somebody who knows that talk alone means nothing. In the photo accompanying the post he is seen taking the knee. The Briton described his sponsorship of an under-23 rider – name yet to be announced – to race for his old Hagens Berman Axeon team this summer as something that is "[hopefully] the beginning of a joint effort to increase racial diversity" in the sport. He deserves every bit of the praise he has received since making the announcement.

However, there is a stark contrast between Geoghegan Hart's words and actions and those of his Ineos Grenadiers team; an outfit which, despite their sizeable budgets since their Sky days, have never followed through on the notion of running a women's team. At its most cynical, this would have been a relatively inexpensive but easy PR win for the organisation. Done properly it would have had a transformative effect on the women's peloton.

Then there's the continued employment of Gianni Moscon, who famously served a six-week suspension after racially abusing Kévin Reza at the 2017 Tour de Romandie. As commendable as the team's promotion of Sky's Rainforest and Ocean Rescue initiatives was, Geoghegan Hart has arguably done more in the past day or so to attempt to right cycling's wrongs than the team has since 2010.

That is no fault of the British rider whatsoever. But when he has to act as a *de facto* lone wolf, it only serves to reiterate how much more work cycling has to do. Geoghegan Hart has received some, thankfully minimal, criticism for taking the knee. Given the historical response from a minority of fans to the team's other Grand Tour winners, perhaps we'll see them switch from dressing up as needles and inhalers to merely holding signs saying

WOKE as a way of showcasing their dislike of Geoghegan Hart from the roadside? I know one thing: having ill-informed social media users accuse him of supporting a "Marxist organisation" seems more appealing than, say, Chris Froome's experience of having piss thrown in his face.

Watching both Geoghegan Hart's and the team's next steps will be fascinating. Will Ineos leverage their sponsorship of the Mercedes F1 team to push this social agenda with Lewis Hamilton, another athlete leading the charge for inclusivity in his sport? What of Moscon's role within the team? How does his past square off against his team-mate's work? Other riders have liked and commented on Geoghegan Hart's social media post but how many will actually join him in speaking out? Based on the shambolic, tokenistic gesture of solidarity with Kévin Reza and the Black Lives Matter movement during last year's Tour de France final stage, expectations are understandably low.

Look, I get it. Cycling is a gruelling sport, requiring the toughest physical and mental minds. Careers are often short, contracts even shorter, and we're never far away from high-profile sponsors pulling out. Job security among many professionals is modest, the risk of injury every time they race is high. But given Matteo Trentin's revelation that fewer than 20 riders out of approximately 800 recently downloaded the CPA's documents outlining potential UCI rule changes and safety measures, something that directly impacts them, the chances of the sport's leading athletes leading the charge for social change seems small.

But whereas Jordan's business rationale showed somebody who both wanted to transcend the sport and was already planning his post-retirement life, the organisational structure of cycling should lend itself to being a hotbed of activism. For a start it's less tribal – fan allegiances rarely lie with a single team. There aren't worries about alienating supporters and struggling to sell season tickets or corporate boxes. Replica jerseys aren't the must-have clothing item. Nor do they have the same personalisation as they do in other sports, so you're unlikely to see Ineo fans doing what some NFL supporters did to their Colin Kaepernick jerseys once he started kneeling during the pre-game national anthem. Furthermore, since a certain Texan's demise nearly a decade ago, no rider has come close to creating a worldwide brand for themselves. Surely it's a lot easier to stand up for what you believe in when there's no ulterior motive to selling yellow bands and concealing the truth?

Geoghegan Hart accepts that he can only control his own actions. He accepts the grim truth, the harsh reality that his voice doesn't "have all the answers" and that his influence is "small". Regardless of how much we admired his ride at last year's Giro, a 360-word post on *Instagram* this week could well define the Londoner's cycling career.

50 METRES FROM GLORY

By Nick Bull, March 19 2021

For somebody who has never done it, the idea of racing nearly 300 kilometres in a single day seems incomprehensible. So the thought of coming so close to winning a race over that distance, a victory that would have been career-defining, and still being able to speak positively about that experience is definitely something I cannot relate to. For Jürgen Roelandts, however, that's his reality.

Five years on from being beaten – somewhat controversially as it later emerged – by Arnaud Démare on the Via Roma, he still takes great pride in coming third at Milan-San Remo. "It was a good day… a good day," he said. "I don't regret anything. I have mostly nice memories and with 50 metres to go I thought I had it. I thought I was going to win San Remo."

Having raced at WorldTour level for 13 consecutive seasons, Roelandts is now enjoying his first year of retirement. During his career he placed in the top five twice at San Remo, Flanders (third in 2013 behind Fabian Cancellara and Peter Sagan), the world championships road race, E3 and Scheldeprijs. "All results that I can be proud of," he said.

But he knows that his life may have played out differently had he crossed the line first on 19 March 2016. Not only would it have been his eighth professional victory (including the national road race title he claimed in 2008), but he would have become the first Belgian to win *La Primavera* since 1999.

"Of course I didn't do my career for those reasons, but I think I would have been very popular in Belgium. Yes, it would have changed things. To win a Monument was a career goal, just like it is for a lot of people in my country. For me to do that, it would have been at Flanders, Paris-Roubaix or San Remo. I came close on this day and I had some other chances after this race – fifth in San Remo two years later when [Vincenzo] Nibali was really strong and won solo – but now I've retired I know that this was my best shot."

Roelandts was three years removed from his last victory, a stage of the Tour Méditerranéen, going into the 2016 race. "I came from Tirreno where I had felt really good. This made me confident. Also, in the previous years in San Remo I had felt strong at the end of the race and I was always in the front group but something went wrong. In 2013 when the group [including eventual winner Gerald Ciolek, Fabian Cancellara and Peter Sagan] went on the Poggio, [Philippe] Gilbert and I missed it by maybe five seconds. Then in 2015 I waited too long to start my sprint, I was trapped and it was too late."

Despite his so-near-yet-so-far moments, Roelandts is still fond of the race. "I always liked the explosive final – Cipressa, downhill, Poggio, downhill, the finish. A lot of this is in the mind. When you go onto the Poggio it's a mental race. Everybody is tired but you need to fight for position. If you think in your head that your legs are tired, you are going to turn on to the climb in 20th or 30th position and it is going to be really difficult. But if you make the extra effort early on and ride the climb in the top five, maybe top 10 positions, the first two kilometres are so much easier. You take your speed with you and you don't have to brake, start, brake, start so much. I'm not the best climber but I learned this over the years."

Watching the race back, Roelandts navigated the race's two noted climbs perfectly. He was never far away from then-world champion Sagan or Cancellara on the Cipressa, and he can be seen towards the head of the peloton with team-mates Jens Debusschere and Tony Gallopin on the Poggio.

"Jens – who is also my brother-in-law – was riding his first Milan-San Remo that day," Roelandts recalled. "He was also my room-mate and before the race we agreed that we would talk about our strategy if we both made it to the top of the Poggio before 15th position. We made it to the top in the peloton and he was in my wheel so I called him. I said I felt really good and that I would do the sprint – I asked him to drop me into [Nacer] Bouhanni's wheel."

Despite the attempts of Edvald Boasson Hagen and Greg van Avermaet, who attacked approaching the *flamme rouge*, the race came down to the sprint Roelandts was seeking. "If you're in the final, you're in a bit of a tunnel," he said, referring to the effects of sprinting after 300 kilometres. Passing through the elongated left/right chicane around Via Fiume he was positioned exactly where he wanted to be, behind Bouhanni.

Then, as if to prove that luck was working in his favour, when Fernando Gaviria fell after touching van Avermaet's wheel, Debusschere, Bouhanni and Roelandts all managed to avoid the Colombian despite being immediately behind him. "It was a bit of a mess with the crash," said Roelandts. "[Avoiding] it was all about my reflex. I was in automatic pilot mode. I remember trying to avoid touching the brakes because I would have lost so much speed. After such a long day, braking there would have been the end of the race, so I just launched."

Roelandts started his sprint a little over 300 metres out from the line. He had to go the long way round to pass van Avermaet, before he settled on a line on the right side of the road. While he was establishing a small gap, Bouhanni slipped a gear, eliminating the Frenchman. Another slice of good fortune, check.

"It was a long sprint and there was a headwind, but with the chaos I just went for it," said Roelandts. "Yes, I know it was long, but I thought that I would make it. I could see the line and I thought that I would make it." It wasn't to be: Démare edged ahead of him 50 metres from the line, before Sky's Ben

Swift benefitted from the Frenchman's tow to take second. "I was really happy with my third place but with some rumours that came afterwards I was a bit disappointed."

Démare found himself in the middle of a short-lived row as riders – most notably Italian's Matteo Tosatto and Eros Capecchi – accused him of taking a tow from a team car on the Cipressa having been delayed by a crash shortly before the climb. Without any video or photographic evidence the result stood, while Démare has always denied any wrongdoing.

One thing that looked slightly off was the case of the Frenchman's Strava file. When first uploaded and compared to other riders, it showed that Démare closed down a gap to the peloton of approximately 40 seconds over the course of the Cipressa ascent and descent. The data was promptly deleted and then uploaded again. Second time around it showed that he had set the KoM on the Cipressa as well as recording the fastest Cipressa to San Remo segment that had been uploaded to the site at the time.

Understandably, this topic still wrangles with Roelandts to this day. He said: "[Démare] was on the car when he had the best time up the Cipressa. He crashed before it, he has the best Strava as a non-climber up the Cipressa, then afterwards he deleted the file. That's something… I think it would have made a difference. If he wasn't there I win San Remo – Swift only passed me with half a wheel on the line and he came in the slipstream."

He admits to having re-watched the ending of the 2016 San Remo fairly recently – "it took me a long time" – and even with the "towing" controversy the extent of his satisfaction with that day's ride is apparent. Roelandts said: "For the first and only time in my career I was the first rider in the peloton at the top of the Cipressa and then the first rider for all of the downhill. This is a nice memory. Of course I could have done better than third but I live with it. It was a good day… a good day."

QUEEN OF THE MUR: ANNA VAN DER BREGGEN ON LIFE AFTER RACING

By Amy Jones, April 22 2021

After her seventh consecutive win at Flèche Wallonne on Wednesday, it's safe to say that Anna van der Breggen is the undisputed 'Queen of the Mur'. The reigning World and Olympic champion has defended her title on the climb every year since 2015. Next year, however, she will be in the convoy as a team manager rather than in the peloton as a rider.

Van der Breggen has known since last year what her transition from life as a rider will look like. The team announced their intention to retain both her and her compatriot, Chantal van den Broek Blaak, as *directrices sportives* after retirement. For many, transitioning out of the sport triggers something of an identity crisis and few receive support.

However, speaking on the eve of Flèche Wallonne, van der Breggen said, "to already know that you will be a sports director next year gives a good feeling that it's not like the black hole of 'I don't know what I'm going to do now.' In your free time you can think about it already and prepare it a bit. So yeah, it's a really nice thing."

If she is able to pass on just a fraction of her prowess to the riders she directs, then team SD Worx look set to continue to rise in 2022 even with van der Breggen absent from the rider roster. "I think it's a really good way of still being in the sport," she says. "The knowledge you have is not a waste. I can teach young girls the things they want to know from me. And that's a really nice thing to do."

The "young girls" have already shown their precocious strength during the Ardennes so far, with 24-year-old Demi Vollering taking second in Amstel Gold and providing a crucial ally for van der Breggen in the final of Flèche Wallonne. Likewise, both Anna Shackley and Niamh Fisher-Black – 19 and 20 years old respectively – put in enormous shifts at the front of the peloton in both races. Along with 21 year-old Dutch talent Lonneke Uneken and new signing Kata Blanka Vas they are destined to go far under van der Breggen's guidance.

For now, though, she is still very much a rider. "It's not affecting the way I approach the season because I'm still in my last season. So I'm a rider and I'm still enjoying it a lot," she says. "I really made the decision that I don't want to be a sports director already because I need to focus on riding very well, training well. But of course, it's affecting things because I think already, in the way other young girls look to me, they know I will be their DS next year."

Although it might not be her primary focus just yet it is certainly on her radar, especially if teammate and fellow future DS van den Broek Blaak is around. "We talk about it, if I'm with Chantal in the room, for example," she says. "I'm looking forward [to it], but it's also still far away."

Van der Breggen and van den Broek Blaak will be under the tutelage of SD Worx manager and director, Danny Stam, who has guided the team through huge success over the years. This season, van der Breggen has been paying careful attention to how Stam executes his job in preparation for her turn. "I think you look different at things, maybe more to the role Danny has now. How do you have meetings? What do you need to have as a sports director? Of course you think about it."

Before she swaps the saddle for the driver's seat, however, there is still the small matter of the 2021 season to contend with, including the Olympics. "I am very aware of enjoying it now as a rider, because I still can, and next year that's over. That's a new chapter." If van der Breggen's racing so far this year is anything to go by, all signs are pointing to her ending on a high.

Chapter Two: The Classics

TIMELINE

February 27: Anna van der Breggen and Davide Ballerini triumph at Omloop Het Nieuwsblad

March 6: Strade Bianche falls to Chantal van den Broek-Blaak, and Mathieu van der Poel

March 16: Tadej Pogačar adds Tirreno-Adriatico to his win in the UAE Tour

March 20: Jesper Stuyven attacks in the last kilometre to take Milan-San Remo

March 21: Trofeo Alfredo Binda ends in a lone win for Elisa Longo-Borghini

March 28: Marianne Vos and Wout van Aert triumph at Ghent-Wevelgem in Flanders Fields

April 1: cancellation of the inaugural women's Paris-Roubaix and the men's race, scheduled for April 11

April 4: at the Tour of Flanders, Annemiek van Vleuten wins solo while Kasper Asgreen outwits van der Poel in the finish sprint

April 18: in Amstel Gold, Vos and van Aert make it another Jumbo Classic double

April 21: a magnificent seventh Flèche Wallonne win for Anna van der Breggen; the men's world champion, Julian Alaphilippe, ditches his rainbow jersey hoodoo

April 25: Pogačar becomes the first rider to win the Tour followed by Liège-Bastogne-Liège since Bernard Hinault in 1980; abetted by van der Breggen, a breakthrough win for Demi Vollering gives SD Worx a fourth Classic.

STRADE BIANCHE: A MONUMENT IN THE MAKING

By William Fotheringham, March 4 2021

From a bike racing perspective, Covid-19 messed up the seasons good and proper in 2020, which meant that the first sighting of the phrase "Strade Bianche should be a Monument" was not a harbinger of spring, but a marker of high summer. This year, though, well done to men's world champion Julian Alaphilippe for getting in there early. Spring is here. The daffodils are nodding. The birds are being noisy. The dust is about to fly on the *sterrate*. And Strade Bianche should be a Monument.

The phrase trips easily off the lips of the commentators and flies across the Twitter feeds. If it does, that speaks justifiably of the highest praise for a race that has established itself in heads and hearts in a matter of a few years, more rapidly than I can remember any other new bike race doing in the 40 years (gulp) since I started to follow the sport. This is only the fifth edition in the WorldTour.

However, it's worth pausing for a moment and asking ourselves what a Monument is, or should be, in bike racing terms, because it's not that long since the whole question of what and where one day races should be and how they should be ranked was put up for grabs. And it's worth doing this only with a proviso: we all have our individual feelings about which races matter to us, for different reasons.

No one seems to be sure when the term was first coined to describe the five biggest one day races in the sport. I'm happy to be corrected, but I don't recall it being used much before the last 20 years at least. My sense is that it is used specifically because the five great one day races, and the Tour de France are the time-honoured poles in the season, fixed at very specific dates in the year, which form the starting point when the cycling calendar is devised. Like Stonehenge or the Colosseum, their historic status is always respected.

So my first criterion for "Monument status" would be the strongest possible sense of time in the narrative of the cycling year: Lombardy effectively closes the season, Milan-San Remo opens it. Paris-Roubaix is the second Sunday in April. The Tour of Flanders is the week before Roubaix. Liège is the week after Roubaix – in my view it should be that way every year, not alternate seasons, because the one point about a Monument, in bike racing terms, is you shouldn't be wondering when it takes place, and it should feel like something is wrong with the world if it isn't at the time it should be. Which is one good reason why 2020 was so totally discombobulating.

Time is my first measure. Place is my second. All five Monuments have the strongest possible identity in terms of their location, to the extent that certain relatively small stretches of road – Arenberg, Poggio, La Redoute, Ghisallo – have become fixed points as well. San Remo, Roubaix and Liège can't really finish anywhere else. Flanders and Lombardy are more movable but organisers mess with this at their peril. Lombardy went through a frightful period when it finished on an anonymous industrial road outside Monza in the 90s, and it regained its identity when it returned to the most traditional finale, the small hills leading into Como; I couldn't help feeling something of the essence of Flanders was lost when it was shifted to a circuit.

In place terms, it goes without saying that Strade Bianche scores higher than many other races, probably as highly as the five Monuments. Those white roads feel unique. But that protected status in the calendar is meant to ensure something else for the Monuments: the best possible field. Strade Bianche clashes with Paris-Nice, still seen, just about, as a build-up race for Milan-

San Remo, so let's see how many of the best Classics riders have opted to race in France. More than you'd think: Mads Pedersen, Matteo Trentin, Arnaud Démare, Yves Lampaert, Michael Matthews. You can't imagine any of that bunch missing San Remo or the Tour of Flanders. However, given the rate at which Strade Bianche has gained stature, who'd bet against every Classic specialist riding it before too much longer?

On top of time, place, and quality of field, you can argue distance and history. Strade Bianche can afford to be shorter than the Monuments and Ghent-Wevelgem, because the off-road quotient is so demanding. If Paris-Roubaix could include 63km of cobbles, up hill and down dale and as long as the *sterrate* sections, it could arguably be run at under 200km as well. History is debatable too. Flanders became international only in the 1950s when the Italians turned up, and Liège was in deep trouble due to organisational issues as recently as the 1980s. Other races than the five Monuments have distance, or used to, and plenty of others have history. History and distance didn't save Bordeaux-Paris or the Championship of Zurich.

History matters in another way. In the early 90s, the UCI head Hein Verbruggen had a go at creating a season-long World Cup, that was intended to take the sport international. That involved inventing Classics in countries outside the European heartland, in a half-assed way, but it also entailed chopping the distance out of non World Cup races such as Ghent-Wevelgem. Races like the Championship of Zurich, Paris-Brussels and Paris-Tours never truly regained their stature after this experiment. Official or not, the designation of the Big Five as Monuments feels like a reaction to this: you mess with their date or location at your peril.

Strade Bianche will be the first encounter this year between the Holy Trinity of Julian Alaphilippe, Wout van Aert and Mathieu van der Poel so it should be a mighty battle. It could also turn out to be the start point for a narrative that could define the 2021 men's racing season. It feels on a par with Classics such as Wevelgem, Het Nieuwsblad, Flèche or Amstel. But it doesn't yet feel like a race where all the one day specialists are saying, "I can't possibly miss that. It has to be on my schedule," and personally I don't think, "it's Strade Bianche, it must be the first weekend in March." It didn't feel out of season in its August slot last year in the way that the Tour of Lombardy did – there was still plenty of dust and dirt in the one, no falling leaves in the other.

Finally, Strade Bianche – men's and women's – should be placed at the heart of a whole officially designated series of partly off-road one day events, based on dirt tracks not cobbles. You could add into it races like Tro Bro Léon, Ghent-Wevelgem (those Plugstreets), CicleClassic, Dwars door het Hageland, and maybe Paris-Tours with its vineyard tracks. I don't know what you'd call the series – "the dust epics" maybe – but to me, right now, that's where the *sterrate* should be given their place rather than among those immutable Monuments.

FOLLOWING TRADITION: TROFEO BINDA PROVES THAT WOMEN'S PELOTON CAN GO THEIR OWN WAY

By Amy Jones, March 22, 2021

Last weekend couldn't have gone any better for Trek-Segafredo, who took the win in both Milan-San Remo with Jasper Stuyven and Trofeo Alfredo Binda with Elisa Longo-Borghini – both in spectacular style. An exciting double-header weekend of racing in Italy, with standalone races for the men and women, proved that the women's calendar does not need to follow the men's model in order to succeed and grow.

On Saturday, some may have wondered why there isn't a women's Milan-San Remo when, increasingly, there are women's editions of many classic men's races. Those wondering, however, may not have been aware of Trofeo Alfredo Binda, the longest established standalone women's one-day race on the calendar – which this year marked its 46th edition.

Standalone women's races such as Binda are one of the few pieces of history unique to the women's peloton. Compare the number of editions of any men's Classic to a women's race and it becomes evident that when events speak of their long tradition they are referring only to the men's race.

Indeed, hosting women's races separately might actually prove more lucrative and garner even greater exposure, according to the CEO of Flanders Classics, Tomas Van den Spiegel, who took to Twitter to lay out the challenges his organisation faces in the wake of a backlash over prize money at one of their races, Omloop Het Nieuwsblad.

As part of a lengthy thread, Van den Spiegel commented: "When it comes to sponsorship it is not an easy job to sell the women's races separately, given the fact that they ride mostly the same course on the same day as their male counterparts. In an ideal future the women's race is a popular standalone event on a different day."

A women's Milan-San Remo would not only be unnecessary, a women's version of Milan-San Remo that took place on the same day as the men's would not work logistically, even at a reduced distance. Not only would the men's coverage eat into the women's, but not even the most dedicated cycling fan wants to sit in front of the television for one second longer once Milan-San Remo is over.

San Remo is a purist's race, steeped in a long tradition. Many have compared it to Test cricket in that it requires the patience and obscure knowledge that would confuse a casual viewer but make it thrilling to those who are privy to the nuances of the sport. Men's cycling can afford this level of obfuscation, but the women's side of the sport is still vying to be seen as a profitable venture – or just to be seen at all. There is constant action in a women's race that a passing viewer would understand; in contrast, there exists a website entitled *ismilansanremoexcitingyet.com* which is itself an in-joke.

Women's racing is explosive and aggressive, which makes every second exciting to watch, a significant reason for this being the shorter distances the women's peloton covers compared to the men's. A race like Milan-San Remo is the antithesis of that. Alfredo Binda, at 141.8km long, lends itself to the style of women's racing with its constant attacks and long-range solo hit-outs. In contrast, San Remo, at 299km, speaks to the tradition of men's cycling wherein fans revel in the 'challenge' of a protracted lead-in to an explosive finish. That's not to say that either one is superior, it's simply a case of horses for courses.

While the women's side of the sport benefits, to an extent, from leveraging the ready-made popularity of races like Paris Roubaix and Flanders, if it is to grow, it also must create its own legend, and Trofeo Alfredo Binda is very much a part of that.

IN FLANDERS FIELDS

By Peter Cossins, March 28 2021

Standing in the mixed zone at Paris-Nice one morning earlier this month, I listened in to *FloBikes* reporter Gregor Brown as he quizzed Classics specialists about the key points on the Ghent-Wevelgem route, focusing particularly on the Plugstreets gravel sections and, of course, the race's totemic climb, the Kemmelberg.

It was fascinating to hear the likes of Oliver Naesen, Sep Vanmarcke, Matteo Trentin and Jasper Stuyven describing the specific challenges of what was once very much a Classic where the sprinters once dominated, but has become more unpredictable in recent seasons, and a far better spectacle.

The general take from the riders was that the Plugstreet sections, which come between the final two of three ascents of the Kemmelberg, don't add much in terms of the overall difficulty of the challenge at this long-standing Classic. The critical thing, according to Trentin, is to get through them without puncturing because waiting for a wheel or a bike and then accelerating back up to the bunch as it's accelerating towards the climbs of the Monteberg and, soon after, the Kemmelberg, is sure to take a toll when the race reaches the latter.

The riders were almost unanimous that the Kemmelberg isn't as iconic as the *bergs* in the Flemish Ardennes a few dozen kilometres to the east, largely because it only features on the route of Ghent-Wevelgem. What's more, they said, the second and final ascent arrives with more than 30km remaining to the finish. Nevertheless, they all agreed, it's a characteristically difficult West Flanders climb thanks to both its cobbled surface and super steep ramps, a place where the race is very unlikely to be won, but which does tend to sort the very best from the rest

That was the case today, when the strongest nine riders coalesced going over the top of it, passing the memorial to the French soldiers who died defending this strategically important hill during the Fourth Battle of Ypres in April 1918.

For me, though, the Kemmelberg is just as iconic as the Flanders *bergs* because of its Great War history. When I first reported on Ghent-Wevelgem during one of the three editions won by Mario Cipollini, I remember driving to see the climb and its memorials the day before the race. I walked up the cobbles, to the top and looked out across the flat plains of Flanders, wondering whether my great-grandfather, Lionel Saynor, had trained his big artillery gun – to which he had been posted after joining up in 1915 – onto its heavily fortified slopes after German forces had captured it the spring of 1918. That autumn, Allied forces took it back again in the Fifth Battle of Ypres, also known as the Battle of the Peaks of Flanders.

Lionel died nine months before I was born, but over the years I've heard stories from my mother about the physical and mental damage he sustained during the First World War, about how he would walk to a certain point in the fields near his East Yorkshire home and then stop, unable to carry on to the "swinging branch" that my mother, then a little girl, wanted to play on. After being rooted to the spot for a while, he'd have to be led back home. The "shell shock", or post-traumatic stress disorder, never went away.

Seeing the riders gathering for the start of Ghent-Wevelgem in Flanders Fields this morning at the Menin Gate, beneath the stone panels featuring the names of more than 54,000 Commonwealth soldiers who died in the battles at Ypres and whose remains were never found, brought Lionel back into my thoughts again. I called my mother, who told me that he'd fought at the Battle of the Somme, earning medals that he refused to accept because, as he often told her, "We were heroes led by donkeys." She didn't know where he was posted after that battle, but we have resolved to find out more.

Later in the day, after watching the riders pass cemeteries with thousands of carefully tended crosses, including the Tyne Cot Memorial to the Missing, I was reminded that one of the unique beauties of bike racing is its constant connection with a landscape that's been shaped by human activity over the centuries. This is what, even in those many moments when not a great deal is happening in the race itself, still makes it captivating and magical. Seeing riders, men and women, of dozens of nationalities racing through this former "hell of the north" is a reason for reflection and even celebration, for realising that things have changed and mostly for the better.

As the riders reached the Kemmelberg for the first time, the action getting gradually more intense and enthralling, it struck me that the same can also be said for Ghent-Wevelgem. Under the aegis of Flanders Classics, it's been thoughtfully revamped and restored. Once stripped down to little more than 200km, it's been beefed back up to full Classics distance and status. Run largely on exposed roads that are raked by the wind, it's always likely to provide a fascinating contest from the off, the racing sometimes better than the Tour of Flanders. The addition of "In Flanders Fields" to its title boosts its importance even more. Today's men's edition highlighted this success of this makeover particularly well, the whittling process beginning very early and continuing all the way into the final dozen kilometres, when Sam Bennett and Danny van Poppel were dropped from the leading group of nine, leaving a very select group of favourites at the front, from which Wout van Aert proved the quickest. Watching the women's race as I write this, the racing is just as engrossing.

It's been a day for memories, sad in parts, exhilarating in others, and ultimately one I won't forget, and that's something that I certainly wouldn't have said about Ghent-Wevelgem a few years ago.

WHY IS FLANDERS SO HARD TO WIN?

By Nick Bull, April 1 2021

The conversation at Trek-Segafredo's dinner table last Sunday night turned away from that afternoon's Ghent-Wevelgem and looked ahead to the fast-approaching Tour of Flanders. "We were looking at the list of former winners," said Ellen van Dijk, one of those involved in the discussion inside a Best Western on the outskirts of Bruges, "and we noticed that there have only been two repeat winners at Flanders."

It's a remarkable stat: the last 12 editions of the Ronde have generated 12 different winners. Ina-Yoko Teutenberg, who retired in 2013 and is now Trek's DS, started this run of different yearly winners in 2009. It is a list that includes the sport's biggest names: Annemiek van Vleuten (2011), Marianne Vos (2013), Lizzie Deignan (2016) and Anna van der Breggen (2018).

But given how some of Flanders' previous champions have been at the forefront of women's cycling over the past decade, how come they've never doubled up at the Ronde? "It's a race with a lot of different opportunities, so maybe that's why," added van Dijk. "In some races you know it's always going to be a bunch sprint, for example, but in Flanders many scenarios can happen and do happen." Additionally, without there being a Milan-San Remo or (until October) Paris-Roubaix equivalent on the women's calendar, its prestige isn't lost on the riders.

"Flanders is the classic of the classics," said Longo Borghini. "Everybody is at their top level. If you're passionate about cycling this race means the world. The history behind Flanders is huge. You feel it during the week: people are warming up. Yes, it was different last year when we could not have the crowds, but normally the atmosphere before race day is like a festival. Passing on the Kwaremont you smell the beer and roasted meat."

Ceratizit-WNT Pro Cycling's Lisa Brennauer, who finished fourth in 2020, agreed with the Trek riders' assessments. "It's special in so many ways. It's constant; cobbled section after cobbled section, climb after climb. And the atmosphere… you cannot help but get into the race as much as the fans do. All these factors give me so much enthusiasm for it. It's a real achievement getting on the podium in this race."

Since the Flanders route was controversially changed in 2012, the Kwaremont – the top of which will fall 16.7 kilometres from the finish in Oudenaarde on Sunday – has been the location of the race-winning move four times. Three successful attacks went in and around the Kruisberg (a little over 25 kilometres out) and one went on the approach to the Paterberg. Van Dijk was the first to win following an acceleration coming off the Kruisberg, helped in part by the element of surprise. "Now everybody expects it," she said. "Everybody is super alert at this point. It's still a very hard point in the race: if you want to make a difference and you're feeling good you can. You know attacks will go here, they just may not be successful."

Coming 126 kilometres into the race, the Kruisberg is where fatigue kicks in, according to Brennauer. "You've come through the town, the race gets strung out, and then comes this cobbled climb. It's a super hard one," said the German rider. "But once you're at the top of it, you turn left, back onto tarmac, and shift into the big chainring. However it's not over there – the road keeps dragging, and it's not so long before you hit the [uncategorised] climb in the woods. To me, it feels like it has become the section where attacks get set up before the race-winning move goes."

Even when Flanders comes down to the Kwaremont, sensing an attack is about to happen is one thing. Responding is another. The helicopter shot used in the television broadcast of van den Broek Blaak's winning move on the false-flat section at the top of the climb last year gave it an appearance of a stealthy acceleration as opposed to an explosive one.

"The Kwaremont is the longest and hardest of the climbs in terms of power," said Brennauer, who was at the head of the reduced front group when the Dutch rider attacked. "It's not as steep as the others but it takes so long to get over it. When she attacked we had already been going so fast already. She came, she had more left and she could go away from us. It was at a moment when everybody was so tired."

Attacking and going clear is one thing. But what happens when you end up in a less than desirable move? The sight of van der Breggen visibly grinning having bridged across to compatriot van Vleuten to neutralise her long-range attack made coming off the Kruisberg in last year's race will be long remembered. The pair have history in the race: despite instigating the four-rider move who broke clear – also over the top of the Kruisberg – in 2017, van der Breggen eventually stopped cooperating with her three escapees: van Vleuten, Longo-Borghini and Kasia Niewiadoma. They were caught under the *flamme rouge*, an outcome Niewiadoma described as "just shit". Justice was served: van den Broek-Blaak, whose presence in the chasing group impacted on van der Breggen's decision to stop taking turns, was beaten into third by Coryn Rivera and Gracie Elvin. Four editions of the race (2012, 2013, 2016 and 2019) have seen small groups come to the line together, illustrating how difficult it is for riders to launch attacks in the 13.2 kilometres that separate the top of the Paterberg and the finish line. Recalling the 2019 edition, in which she and van Vleuten battled it out with Marta Bastianelli for the victory, Uttrup Ludwig admitted she knew her chances of victory were slim. "When I was sitting in that group I did think 'oh shit' because Marta was flying that year. Normally it's not a good idea to come home with a sprinter. There are so many good riders who can survive these short climbs: if you bring Lotte Kopecky or Marianne Vos to the line it's like you're dealing with second or third. If we want to get rid of these super sprinters we have to hope for a super hard race."

Brennauer went into last year's Flanders off the back of consecutive eighth-place finishes in the event. In the sprint for second, she was pipped narrowly by Amy Pieters and Kopecky. "This finish – it's really a pain," she joked. "You see the line for such a long time because it's on a straight road. You have to tell yourself to wait and open the sprint at the right time. But you're already so tired it's almost impossible to turn your pedals around."

The *Ronde* is arguably cycling's biggest numbers game, too. Four of the last seven editions have seen teams claim one-twos (Boels-Dolmans in 2014, 2018 and 2020; Wiggle Honda in 2015), while Boels took an arguably even more impressive one-three-four-six in 2016. "I think your chances decrease when you don't have a super strong team," said Uttrup Ludwig. "You have to choose which attacks you follow [when you're alone] and sometimes it's luck that you choose the right one. But you want to be on the team who can play the numbers."

While van Dijk's palmarès may list a single Flanders victory, history needs to record the role she played in both Deignan's and Rivera's triumphs. Her pacesetting on the Kwaremont weakened the Briton's rivals and set up her attack en route to the Paterberg five years ago; she then helped chase down the four-rider move in 2017 that produced an anomalous bunch sprint from which Rivera became the first American winner of the race.

"It's really nice when you can give something back for somebody," van Dijk said. "The year I won, Lizzie was my back-up. She was there for the sprint if I was caught, so it was nice that I could do the Kwaremont at a high pace for her in 2016. When Coryn won, I didn't have my good climbing legs that day so I couldn't follow on the Kwaremont. But then afterwards I closed the gap back to the first [chasing] group. I knew that I could still play a big role in the race. My thinking wasn't like 'I couldn't go with the best riders, it's all done'. Situations can happen, especially with the long straight to the finish. I like time trialling so I was in my comfort zone."

There's one more factor that has impacted on Flanders in recent years but arguably applies across the entire calendar: the quality of riders in the women's peloton. "The minimum wage has really helped," said Uttrup Ludwig. "More people can live off cycling now, instead of riders working next to cycling. Back in the day when I was standing [and working] in a supermarket… that's not super good for recovery." Van Dijk agreed, adding: "The level and depth is getting bigger. These days the wins are getting divided up – the four WorldTour races so far have all had different winners. It's so unpredictable."

IS THIS THE RETURN TO THE AGE OF ANNEMIEK?

By Amy Jones, April 5 2021

Annemiek van Vleuten is now the second rider in history to have won the Tour of Flanders twice at a ten year interval. The 38-year-old Dutch rider took the victory in 2011, and again on Sunday. It was her second win in five days – following Dwars door Vlaanderen on Wednesday – but the European champion didn't have the start to the 2021 WorldTour campaign that we had come to expect of her.

Van Vleuten was looking unassailable last season, coming out swinging in 2020 wearing the rainbow stripes and maintaining a 100% winning record between February and August – albeit with racing on hiatus in between. Later, she looked set to win the Giro Rosa for the third consecutive year before crashing out of the race. A second place at the world championships in Imola – with a broken wrist – followed by a somewhat lacking latter half of the year closed out her final season with Mitchelton-Scott, the team she had raced with for five years.

Watching van Vleuten clip off the front of a race and time trial her way to the finish has become a recurring image in women's racing in recent seasons. The former world time trial champion usually waits until the hardest point in the race before making her move, usually never to be seen again before the finish.

However, the start of the 2021 season was different, punctuated by consecutive victories and near wholesale domination from newly-rebranded SD Worx (formerly Boels Dolmans) with myriad champions past and present on their roster. The team looked like they had returned to the Boels Dolmans of 2016-18, winning the first two WWT races and cleaning up in the lower categories too. So far this season, the team has had six wins from six different riders.

Meanwhile, van Vleuten, in her new home, Movistar, looked like she was struggling to adapt. She missed a crucial split in Omloop Het Nieuwsblad and where once she made closing down a huge gap at Strade Bianche look easy, she was barely anywhere to be seen this time around. Clearly noticing something was missing, she took herself off to Tenerife for some altitude training, skipping the next two rounds of the WorldTour. Fittingly, her closest rival, current world champion Anna van der Breggen, also opted out of the same race period to train in the high mountains.

In the pair's absence, the racing continued to be as aggressive and unpredictable as women's racing so often is. Trek-Segafredo appeared to pick up the mantle from a waning SD Worx with Elisa Longo Borghini winning Trofeo Alfredo Binda off the back of a textbook team effort.

Noticeably this season, in the second year of a mandated minimum salary for WorldTour teams, more squads are riding cohesively as teams than ever before rather than one or two stronger riders navigating their way alone. Liv Racing and FDJ Nouvelle Aquitaine Futuroscope are prominent examples. Who knew that paying riders a living wage allows them to become better riders?

It's easy to overstate van Vleuten's dominance over the peloton. Her racing – often deservedly – invites hyperbole, yet she is not unbeatable. If the *parcours* isn't tough enough or she isn't able to deploy her trademark solo breakaway then she is no more likely to win from a bunch than anyone else. At both Dwars door Vlaanderen and Flanders, she didn't completely steam-roll the rest of the bunch as she has in the past.

At Dwars door Vlaanderen, Kasia Niewiadoma of Canyon// SRAM pulled off a feat that was seemingly impossible in seasons past as she latched onto van Vleuten's wheel and held it to the line. Likewise, at Flanders, although van Vleuten did shake off the rest of the group to take yet another solo victory, it was with a much smaller margin than she's been used to.

The dominant Dutchwoman might have won the last two races she started but the peloton are not only savvy to her tactics, they are now more capable of countering them. Whether it's the result of a shorter off-season or added depth as a result of (steadily) increasing professionalisation, the rest of the peloton are coming up to meet her and the racing is all the better for it.

THE GREAT ROUBAIX DEBATE: WET AND SLIPPY OR DRY AND DUSTY?

By William Fotheringham, April 11 2021

The 2021 cobbled Classics season ended not with bangs, clatters and a few curses, but with a whimper of frustration and the gentle pitter-patter of rain falling on northern France. It won't be the highest up the list of things that I feel deprived of due to Covid-19, but it's been frustrating to watch the weather reports for Lille and environs and ponder that we might, finally, have had the wet Paris-Roubaix we have been waiting for since Servais Knaven's mudspattered win in the gloop of 2001.

Which brings me to the big question. The one which comes up every April, until the point where we all realise that, yet again, Paris-Roubaix is going to be DND (dry'n'dusty) rather than WNS, (wet'n'slippery). Which is actually better: the wet Roubaix most connoisseurs seem to want, or the dry one is what we always have to put up with? And what is the actual difference, given it's been so long since we saw the cobbles soaked and muddy?

Not everyone wants a wet Roubaix, of course. Since publishing my "biography" of Jørgen Leth's iconic film *A Sunday in Hell*, I've set up numerous screenings of the film around the UK (the blasted pandemic robbed us of last spring's of course) and when we do Q&A afterwards, one thing is always asked: was Leth frustrated by the fact that the edition he shot of Roubaix, the 1976 race, was DND not WNS?

Leth told me that, contrary to what one might imagine – don't we all love those images of riders covered in gunk, red-rimmed eyes peering through the mudpack? – he preferred to have a DND edition to work with. The dust is one factor. The great clouds of it billowing across the course like gunpowder smoke at a battle give him magnificent material – those helicopter shots, those images of bike riders and team cars emerging from the miasma to that insane chorale.

There was also the fact that for Leth, a dry Paris-Roubaix was far better for his cameramen to work in, reducing the chances that things would go wrong technically. But most importantly, perhaps, in 1976 a dry Hell of the North made for a better narrative: the favourites stayed together for longer, the winning break took longer to form, and it stayed together until the finish, meaning that the race was not decided until the final metres.

Which is where I start wondering about the WNS or DND conundrum. The irony is that on the wettest, nastiest day I can recall in "Hell" in recent years, in the 1994 Roubaix, the narrative wasn't that interesting. It was obvious that Andrei Tchmil was going to win from about 50km out. The most intriguing, suspenseful Roubaix of recent years, the completely mad 2016 edition, was dry. And dusty. Won by Matt Hayman, the race was made by Tom Boonen, who raced in a gloriously devil take the hindmost fashion.

For sure, the wet makes a difference. The fact that the riders are more likely to crash is delicately balanced against the fact that they are travelling more slowly over the cobbles. It was Marc Madiot who said this week that the trouble with a dry Roubaix is that the riders hit the sections at 45kph. Is it harder to see team cars through a dust cloud or through a pile of wet mud? Hard call.

Technically it's a different challenge, because the option of riding on the dirt at the pave edge is not there, and there are puddles to dodge, but is it "better" racing? Hard call. It's well known that when it's wet, the riders keep further apart, due to the flying gloop and the lack of margin for error: it's physically more demanding because drafting is less of a factor, but that's not better, necessarily. An Alpine climb is physically more demanding than any in the Basque Country, but Itzulia looked pretty damn exciting this week.

My perfect Roubaix remains the 1994 edition. When it rained for weeks in northern France, the cobbles were drenched, and it snowed as they pulled out of Compiègne at the start. When Tchmil made his escape there were no motorbike cameras there to capture the moment, I seem to recall, because all the motorbikes had crashed on the insanely slippery mud, and were trying to catch up. The way I see it, cycling is pretty crazy as a sport. Paris-Roubaix is the craziest race that sport boasts. And a wet Paris-Roubaix is the craziest of the crazy. If you like cycling because it's extra-ordinary, well, you have to love a wet Paris-Roubaix.

So, rain or drought? WNS or DND? Well, personally I'd always thought I'd go for WNS. But I have a horrible suspicion that that's actually not for any practical reasons, but because every year I have an idealised view of Paris-Roubaix that I hope will come along, and in my mind's eye, that view stems from images of Kelly, Madiot, Moser and Kuiper, covered in mud, slipping and sliding through the gloop. The Hells of my youth, mainly captured by Graham Watson for *Winning* magazine. My favourite image? Walter Godefroot covered in yick, from *Miroir du Cyclisme*. The Tchmil and Knaven editions of Roubaix fit that paradigm.

However, I have recently come to a horrible suspicion that I want to see a wet Roubaix mainly because most years that's what I don't get to see. And the truth is, of course, that after the last couple of editions have failed to materialise, I've realised I don't much care any more whether it rains or not in the second week of April in northern France. I'd take any kind of Paris-Roubaix right now, wet or dry.

HAYMAN'S HEAVENLY DAY IN HELL

By Sophie Smith, April 15 2021

Out of all the Monuments, there is a case to be made that Paris-Roubaix is the grandest. The unreserved, collective disappointment last week when the 2021 edition was again postponed amid the Covid-19 pandemic attests as much. People shared screenshots on social media of weather forecasts, despondent that they were not only going to miss Roubaix but a potentially wet Roubaix.

Few if any other race garners such a reaction from the peloton, pundits and fans alike. Mathew Hayman competed in Paris-Roubaix 17 times – the most participations of any Australian – and on the fifth anniversary of his 2016 triumph, an upset win in which he denied Tom Boonen a record-breaking fifth title, he reflects on why he was so, like many others, affected by the race.

"I'm not really sure how Roubaix ended up being my favourite race. It definitely is and that was long before I won it," says Hayman, who is now working as a DS at BikeExchange. "I came over from the amateurs and I remember really fighting pretty hard to get my first start there, needing to perform in the other classics to get a start. Flanders at that time was pretty hotly contested. There was always a spot in Roubaix for a neo-pro or a couple of young riders."

Stories from the 'Hell of the North', which traversed northern France near the Belgium border, were intimidating but Hayman replies that the race suited his characteristics, and fans from cycling's traditional homelands were striking.

"You'd heard all the stories made people scared, but then also the crowds and the atmosphere in France there. Getting closer to Belgium, the Belgian fans as well, I remember my first couple of years going through Carrefour de l'Arbre and the amount of beer-breathed Belgians that were yelling at you, it was a tunnel of crowd and fans," he says.

Standing at 1.89m and weighing more than 80kg when he was competing, Roubaix, with its flat roads and sharp, uneven cobblestone sectors through pastures haunted by battlefield soldiers, suited the physical characteristics of the bigger riders in the peloton like him. "There's not many races on the calendar quite like it, so once you find a race like that, that suits your qualities, then you start to enjoy it," Hayman says.

"It's hard but the thing for me was I find a mountain stage in the Tour de France a lot harder because it's not something that I enjoy, it's not something I'm good at. Where for Roubaix, I'm ready to go. That's the one race I want to be at, that's what I've been looking forward to, that's what every training session through November and December has been about. That's why you do the extra kilometres, is to be ready for that race."

My lasting memory of Paris-Roubaix is bumping into Hayman at the 2013 edition, which Fabian Cancellara won. Outside the velodrome I saw Hayman and abruptly asked if we could have a quick chat. Hayman's entire face was covered in an even layer of fine, brown dirt as he gestured towards a nearby car. After almost six hours of racing over jarring cobbles that the peloton sprints to be in position for, he needed something to rest against. He didn't appear quite with it as he spoke. His eyes moved as if he was flicking through a rolodex looking for something important. He appeared to be reliving every point of the race, talking to himself as much as he were to me, so much so that afterwards I questioned whether he'd remember what he said and whether it was therefore ethical for me to report.

"Physically, yeah, of course you're spent at the end of it. You're spent at the end of it because it's also the end of all the [cobbled] Classics and you're spent mentally because it's all done. You get to Roubaix and I think the emotion that comes out in that velodrome is not just about that race, but everybody's Classics campaign done. You're sitting on the grass there and weighing up how it went, the last five or six months of your life being dedicated to those races. You've got a balance sheet there and nine times out of 10 it's pretty disappointing."

ooooo

Hayman forged a long career as a selfless team player who worked in the service of others. In the second half of his career, Roubaix gave Hayman a chance he was otherwise never afforded. "It was the only race of the year where I had a bit of leadership and a protected role where the guys would be helping me. I shied away from being road captain and just focused on myself," he says.

"A lot of pressure was from myself, nobody else. It was for many years a love/hate relationship. A few top 10s there, you know, gave me a glimmer of hope that maybe one day I could be on the podium. And that was always the dream, to end up on the podium in Roubaix."

The distinction Hayman makes between finishing on the podium – not necessarily winning – is a nod to his conditioning as a team player. "Not even in the back of my mind did I think it was possible to win in 2016. In the back of my mind I felt like I could maybe end up on the podium if the race went my way," he says.

The first critical part that year, his 15th appearance, was getting into the early escape with teammate Magnus Cort Nielsen. "I could save energy as far as we didn't really have to sprint for any of the sectors, just rolling over, concentrating on eating and drinking and waiting for the big guys to come," he says. "And I think that was another thing, through my experience, of just knowing that they would come and not trying to make that breakaway go as far as possible, but just being there ready for when the leaders come across."

The second critical point was a realization that he was "actually on a good day". "When Ian Stannard and I came together on Carrefour de l'Arbre I was dropped off the back of the front group there and really felt my race was done. My shoulders slumped and I thought, 'Argh, this is my lot, this is what I deserve,'" he reflects.

"Fighting back on there at the end of that cobble sector and realising that actually I'm not that tired, or I am tired but not as bad as I thought I was, and these guys aren't as strong as I thought they were the sector before, from that point on, I grew in confidence. Being able to get back on, on such a critical, hard sector when Sep Vanmarcke was attacking, that gave me some confidence and from that moment on I started to believe that I was actually on a good day."

ooooo

Hayman began racing in Canberra – Australia's sterile capital city that was founded 11 days before the 18th edition of Paris-Roubaix in 1913. In 2016 he rode into Roubaix in the eye of the storm, bolstered by childhood memories.

"I was surprisingly calm going in there in the lead," he says. "I had grown up in Canberra racing on the velodrome. I'd raced as a junior all the way through to the amateur ranks, so I had a bit of previous form on the velodrome.

"Coming in, look, I could have given it to Tom and just led him out and I would have been probably guaranteed a second place. In hindsight, that was probably the safest thing to do because normally you don't beat Tom in a sprint, and I dreamed about being on the podium," he continues.

"But by the time we came around to the bell [lap] everybody had come back so there was five of us together, with Sep being the first one and then Ian Stannard and [Edvald] Boasson Hagen, who were all fast in their own right."

The team player gave way to the Narrabundah kid racer as Hayman went high up the track. "To be honest it was all just impulsive. I wasn't really thinking, I wasn't really making decisions," he says. "I feel kind of lucky in that defining moment in my career that I was actually not struck by the moment itself and was just racing.

"I felt like I was racing my bike like I thought you were supposed to race. You know, if somebody attacks you go across and you go over the top of them. It's not until I look back that I think how much of it all could have gone wrong. You know, I did hit out early in the sprint, I could have been beaten but at the time it was me having fun, enjoying racing.

"Even into that last bend I was still just thinking about getting on the podium but somewhere deep down I guess letting those other guys back into the race, and not just leading Tom out from a lap out, I was feeling maybe a bit more confident than I thought," Hayman recalls.

"On those bikes with the tyres pretty flat after a hard race, to go high, to get that extra height and length to pass somebody on a velodrome, I knew that if you led out you had an advantage. I could stay low, and the guys were fighting on my wheel and the rest is history."

FLÈCHE WALLONNE: HIDDEN GEM OR UNWORTHY CLASSIC?

By Nick Bull, April 20 2021

Watching Chris Boardman pulling ridiculously long turns during his unsuccessful breakaway attempt at Flèche Wallonne 21 years ago is my oldest and, to this day, one of the most vivid memories I have from the Belgian Classic. Watching the race a few hours after it happened, I can recall my grandfather saying something like "he's either naïve or he's stupid" as Boardman gave breakaway companion Raimondas Rumsas what appeared to be a relatively easy ride throughout their ill-fated bid for glory.

In the Briton's case, it transpired that the 175-kilometre breakaway was actually useful, a training exercise for his Hour Record attempt later that year. But my relative's description of Boardman arguably remains applicable when it comes to Flèche, especially for any male rider attacking anywhere before the 200 metres to go marker on the Mur de Huy. It is 18 years since the men's race was last won by a breakaway winner – Saeco's Igor Astarloa. Unlike, say, Milan-San Remo and Paris-Roubaix, where energy conservation is oft-cited as a key factor in the deciding the outcome, we always hear – and often see – that Flèche is about positioning in the final couple of kilometres and the timing of any acceleration on its steep finishing climb. Ignoring the terrain, that description makes the race sound like a sleepy, flat, first-week Grand Tour stage.

It's a race that does very little for me and many of my peers, at least until the unofficial World Hill-Climb Championship begins. However, many riders still seem to love it. Two-time winner Julian Alaphilippe has called it "a race close to my heart since my [first] participation." Cecilie Uttrup Ludwig, runner-up in 2020, believes it is an "epic race." She added: "You don't win it by coincidence – you win it because you were the strongest rider. It [Mur de Huy] is a mega, mega climb. Everybody knows it's a death climb but I guess you have to have a love-hate relationship with it."

Anna van der Breggen has a less contradictory association with the Mur – "it's a climb I really like," she said last year – having won La Flèche Wallonne Féminine for a record sixth time in a row. While her unbeaten run appears to be under threat owing to a recent illness, half of the Dutchwoman's victories in the race were anything but copies of the formulaic and predictable men's event. In her first three wins in the race (2015, 2016 and 2017), she used the Côte de Cherave, ironically introduced to spice up the men's event, as her launchpad.

But, take away these and Evelyn Stevens' fine tactical victory in 2012, and what are we left with from the race's last 15 years? Where's the Mathew Hayman, Roubaix-style, against-all-odds victory? Or an equivalent of Ellen van Dijk's almighty 27-kilometre solo win at Flanders seven years ago, when Rabo-Liv couldn't close her attack down with four riders in the chase? Nothing in the last decade and a half has come close to the drama of Vincenzo Nibali attacking on the Poggio and holding off the sprinters, as he did in San Remo three years ago, that's for sure. We seek intrigue from cycling, arguably more so in one-day races than Grand Tours. "Why is Kasper Asgreen happy to take Mathieu van der Poel to a sprint finish?" we asked ourselves at the start of April during the Tour of Flanders. Sunday's Amstel Gold Race had us (justifiably) questioning why Elisa Longo Borghini wasn't riding with Kasia Niewiadoma. Sometimes our assumptions are wrong, which I can live with. But, when it comes to Flèche Wallonne, the script very rarely poses these questions.

Of course, Flèche is far from being all bad. The battle for position on the approach to the Mur, followed by the gradual whittling down of the peloton on it, is must-see racing. Because of its long-standing use in the race, the TV production of the finish is normally excellent, not only in capturing the slow-motion sprint, but also showing how steep the climb is. Its roll of honour includes Grand Tour winners, world champions and, er, Dani Moreno, yet it is also easy to remember those who got their tactics wrong and didn't win: Cadel Evans in 2008, Joaquim Rodríguez in 2010 and 2011, Marianne Vos in 2012 and Dan Martin in 2017. Somewhat belatedly, but better late than never, live coverage of the women's race was introduced in 2020.

So, what could be done to improve Flèche? The seemingly obvious answer is extending the race by a kilometre, shifting the finish back onto the N66 road that is already used as part of its finishing circuit. This false flat section would almost certainly change the dynamic of the race; it's also what Thomas De Gendt advocated in 2017. "The race organisers should have the guts to move the line further on," he said. "That would make this Classic more than just a sprint uphill." Sunday's Amstel Gold seemingly validates his point: Longo Borghini and Niewiadoma were the strongest riders on the Cauberg. However, they finished eighth and 10th respectively after being caught by a chasing group on the slightly downhill approach to the line.

I'll admit this is where I'm conflicted. Do we want really another Amstel Gold-style race, especially in the same week? After the finish of Liège-Bastogne-Liège was moved away from its uphill drag onto the Rue Jean Jaurès in Ans two years ago, don't the explosive climbers deserve at least one finish to a Classic that suits them? That only Philippe Gilbert (2011) and van der Breggen (2018) have claimed the Ardennes triple in recent years hints at three nuanced events.

Speaking in 2017, after Alejandro Valverde won a fourth-consecutive edition of the race, Martin disagreed with the idea of amending the finish. "I think the Mur is definitely an art to get right – I just haven't mastered it yet," he said. "I don't think they should change the race so one guy doesn't win. This is the one race that really has a lot of character and it has its trademark. We've seen in years before that races lose their identity when they change too much." He has a point. Could ASO, the race's organiser, really be trusted with such a responsibility, given that their recent attempts at improving racing include Tour de France bonus seconds, that starting grid, and the infamous La Course time trial pursuit around Marseille?

Instead, should those of us historically unmoved by the race try harder to accept Flèche for what it is? Sure, eleven of the last 14 women's editions have been won by van der Breggen and Vos, but dominance is a part of any sport. Is abandoning over 30 years of finishes on the Mur de Huy justified in response to all-time greats delivering unforgettable and unbeatable performances? At a time when some of the leading teams in European football are (rightly) being criticised for trying to create a breakaway Super League, seemingly for the sake of establishing a content and brand-driven entity, perhaps the race's USP and heritage is actually worth fighting for? I think it goes something along the lines of: "Hey, it's a super boring [to quote Tony Martin in 2015] race, but it's OUR super boring race!" Perhaps, to paraphrase my relative, in my ambivalence towards Flèche Wallonne, I'm the one being stupid.

Chapter Three: Ineos Wipe the Floor in Italy

GIRO D'ITALIA TIMELINE

May 8: Filippo Ganna wins the opening time trial in Turin
May 9: Tim Merlier gives Alpecin-Fenix their first Grand Tour stage in Novara
May 10: another Grand Tour first, for Taco van der Horn and Intermarché-Wanty
May 13: Paris-Nice nearly man Gino Mäder takes a popular win at Ascoli Piceno; Attila Valter becomes the first Hungarian to wear the pink jersey
May 16: Egan Bernal begins his run for victory with a stage win at Campo Felice
May 19: Mauro Schmid takes a dramatic stage to Montalcino over the Tuscan *sterrato*
May 22: Lorenzo Fortunato wins the Monte Zoncolan *tappone* for the Eolo-Kometa team
May 23: the stage to Gorizia is stopped in the opening kilometre after a massive crash
May 24: the Cortina stage is curtailed due to bad weather: Bernal wins solo to all but assure overall victory
May 26: Dan Martin joins the select group to win stages in all three Grand Tours with victory at Sega di Ala
May 30: Ganna lands his fifth Giro time trial stage in less than 12 months; Bernal takes the overall

FRENCH HOPES FOR THE PINK JERSEY AS DISTANT AS EVER AS GIRO CLIMBING STAGES GET UNDER WAY

By Jeremy Whittle, May 10 2021

As the 104th Giro d'Italia rolls on deeper into its first week, it does so without a French rider expected to contend for a top three finish. Only a few years ago, French riders were resurgent, poised for glory, with Thibaut Pinot and Romain Bardet regularly figuring among the pre-race favourites for a top three finish on the podium in either Paris, Milan or Madrid. The thought of one of them ending the French Grand Tour drought – the last French overall win was through Laurent Jalabert in the 1995 Vuelta – seemed credible. Not any more.

Pinot is now a disillusioned shell of the rider who sent French fans into a frenzy of expectation in the July of 2019, while Bardet, now sharing Giro leadership at Team DSM with last year's runner-up, Jai Hindley, seems more vague on his career path than ever before. How much of Bardet's repositioning is down to the years of pressure leading a French team, now in his past, allied to the aftermath of his frightening concussion in the 2020 Tour, is hard to tell.

Like Pinot a few years ago, Bardet is now looking to the Giro to reboot his career. "I feel in my element," he said of racing in Italy, as the Giro began. Yet if that is genuinely his intention, he hardly got off to a flying start. His performance in the opening time trial, over 50 seconds down on stage winner Filippo Ganna in the 8.6 kilometres test, was among the worst, even for a rider whose career is littered with time trial fails.

Bardet's time trialling has long been an Achilles heel, however, so no big surprises there, but his attitude to Giro reconnaissance seems even more nonchalant. "We decided not to do any reconnaissance, so I am swinging a little in the unknown," he admitted as the race began in Turin. "I've been to the Dolomites a few times, but I don't know them as well as the Alps or the Pyrenees, that's obvious."

In contrast with the Tour, which Bardet described as often "padlocked," he said that he was "in the mood" for what he described as the "beauty and grandeur" of the Giro. The first real test of just how much Bardet is "in the mood" is likely to come on Tuesday's stage four, a schizophrenic day that goes from flat and rolling to steep and mountainous in the closing hour or two of racing.

The final climb, Colle Passerino, with sections as steep as 16 per cent, may make Bardet wish he had done some reconnaissance, given how infamously eccentric the Giro's road book, the *Garibaldi*, can sometimes be. In reality though, Bardet, like so many others, is hanging on for the final week of the Giro, when the accumulation of brutal and demanding climbs will take their toll.

Yet it feels as if a French Grand Tour win is as distant again as it ever has been, as unlikely even as a British Grand Tour win once was. What has happened to the buoyant French scene then, since Bardet finished second in the 2016 Tour de France? Firstly, it is unfair to pin it all on these two riders. Many others have flattered to deceive, from Thomas Voeckler to Tony Gallopin to Pierre Rolland, and so on. It seems there's always a long line of French riders willing to be this season's Christophe Moreau.

This year, it's likely be either David Gaudu, third in Liège-Bastogne-Liège, or Elie Gesbert, fifth overall in the Tours of Valencia and Algarve, who will bear the burden of Grand Tour expectations, Julian Alaphilippe having wisely removed himself from Tour de France build-up chatter by talking up his hopes for the Tokyo Olympics. The growth in Gaudu's profile has been a long time coming but he is a natural successor to Pinot. It remains to be seen how he will handle the inevitable pressure.

Ask those working in French cycling why, after all the years spent in the wilderness, the nation is now again struggling to find a convincing Grand Tour contender and the responses are not particularly enlightening.

At the beginning of 2020, Pinot's experienced sports director Philippe Mauduit told me: "After the Festina Affair, all the French teams had an excuse – *'tout le monde est dope!'* or 'everyone is doping!' – and the standard of work went down. They reached the point when they had to stop that mentality and rebuild."

"Maybe cycling was still not clean but there was another truth too," he said, "that the French were left behind, they were stuck, blocked, because of Festina. It's not that the past two, three, four years has seen a huge change, but more that all of that rebuilding work is coming good."

Twelve months on, however, at the start of 2021 and plagued by back problems, Pinot himself painted a very different picture. "Cycling still operates at two speeds, I think," he said in a long interview with French daily *L'Equipe*. Explaining his rejection of the use of injections for his back pain, Pinot said: "…you abandon, you play the game, and you do things properly. That's what gets to me most with all of this. You can get angry with the world, but I'll stick to my own thing and I'll finish my career like that."

"There's always a new thing that comes along," he said. "Anyway, I think I'm too anxious, too stressy to mess around with that nonsense. If you told me to take this or that, I wouldn't sleep at night." There's little doubt what the Frenchman was alluding to with those words.

From a distance it looks as if Pinot's glory days are now over, while Bardet's lacklustre time trialling continues to play against him in Grand Tours, which, after a few seasons during which the race of truth was almost absent, are now building kilometres against the clock back into their routes.

The last Frenchman to win the *maglia rosa* was Laurent Fignon, 32 years ago, in spring 1989. Once it looked as if Pinot might succeed him, just as it seemed that Bardet was within touching distance of the *maillot jaune* and possibly, victory in Paris. In another era, maybe they would both have been successful, but whatever the reasons, their chances have gone.

Now, having done no reconnaissance, Bardet is casting his eye around the Giro's hills and mountains, using the beautifully drawn but somewhat eccentric *Garibaldi* as his guide. You don't have to know the Giro very well to know that this may not be the best recipe for success.

BUMPS AND SHUNTS AND LIFE IN THE CONVOY

By Jeremy Whittle, May 14 2021

Until about a decade or so ago, I used to drive a press car in the convoy during major races – that is in among the team cars, TV motorbikes, guest cars, and yes, the bike riders. The peak of this experience would be a stage of the Tour de France, when the intensity of ebb and flow among the vehicles, motorbikes and riders was nerve-racking.

There were often several other press cars in there – jostling with the VIPs, the TV motos, the team cars and the *commissaires*. It was sometimes terrifying and mostly unnecessary. I wasn't filming, just observing. It never really added that much more insight, beyond reinforcing the dangers and brutality of professional road racing.

The last time I drove a Tour stage 'in' the race, my passenger ended up crouched in the foot well, quivering, after a high-speed downhill slalom through a pretty village somewhere in the Auvergne, induced a near panic attack. The next day I decided that maybe I'd had enough of the stress too.

Besides, I felt that driving 'in-race' was getting increasingly dangerous and that there had been enough near-misses. My presence, no matter how good a driver, was just taking up more space. I'd learned an important lesson. When you're alongside another car, close enough to the driver to chat about what they had for dinner last night or to read the screen on their phone, you're probably too close.

A couple of years later, came the infamous and shocking Johnny Hoogerland incident, in which a French television media car sent the Dutchman flying through a barbed wire fence, after the driver misjudged the gap between the breakaway and a gnarled tree.

Thankfully, things are different now. There are far stricter controls on who drives in the convoy and how skilled they are. Luckily most of those who drive in professional bike races are ex-pros who are skilled drivers, operating in a high-pressure environment and under intense scrutiny, much as they did as a professional rider.

When, in full view of live TV cameras, Team BikeExchange sports director Gene Bates shunted Pieter Serry's back wheel towards the end of stage six of the Giro d'Italia, as he pulled alongside a commissaire's car to collect clothing, it was a silly accident caused by a moment's inattention. Serry, who landed hard on the tarmac, was understandably furious, but managed to finish the stage.

Bates will not see Milan. The UCI threw him off the race, while also fining his passenger, fellow sports director and former pro, Matt White, two thousand Swiss francs. There was an outraged reaction to the shunt from social media and some pundits, but really, was it an over-reaction to a banal accident, one of a kind that is much more common in the convoy than some would like to admit?

"Of course we were sorry," White told *lacourseentete.com* on Friday. "It was totally an accident and Gene spent 20 minutes apologising to Peter Serry after the stage. There's no bad blood with Deceuninck Quickstep. They understood it was an accident. We admitted that and understood it was worth a sanction, but not that it was bad enough for Gene to be thrown off the race."

Serry later thanked Team BikeExchange for their apologies, while White added that the squad had protested against Bates' expulsion. "The UCI's head commissaire listened to our arguments and went back to ask, but was told by a higher power that the decision to ban Gene stood. The irony is that it was the commissaires that called us up there in the first place," White said. "They told us they had some rain jackets for us to collect – that was at the bottom of the last climb. We didn't need them then, we'd have happily waited to pick up the jackets until after the stage."

But White also argued that responsibility for improving safety, across the board, applied to all those working on the race. "Twenty four hours before, a Qhubeka-Assos car totalled a Team DSM car, but that wasn't even mentioned in a communiqué and the car's a write off. Isn't safety in the convoy about all of us? Look at the stage finish to Cattolica [in which Mikel Landa was among those who crashed]. Who got sanctioned for that?"

"We have now lost a DS for the whole Giro," White said. "The most hypocritical part of it by the UCI is that they wouldn't reduce it to a five day ban so he could come back on the race later on, but they did say he could go and work on the Tour of Hungary. So it's not a ban from UCI races, it's just a ban from the Giro."

Now, the Australian argued, a precedent has been set. "We asked them what the race ban was based on and they mentioned an incident with a driver of an ambulance a couple of years back, but that's a different situation to a team car working in the convoy."

In fact, over the years there have been numerous incidents of riders being clipped by, or colliding with, in-race vehicles, from Hoogerland's crash, Peter Sagan at the Vuelta, Julian Alaphilippe's tangle with a *moto* during last year's Tour of Flanders, Bob Jungels being sideswiped by an ambulance in last year's Tour de France and so on – once you start totting them all up, it's a very long list.

For Team BikeExchange, racing on many fronts and running a women's team, it's a member of staff that they can ill afford to lose during the second biggest stage race of the season. "We will manage," White said of the loss of Bates. "You can do it with one less DS. We'll still get the work done but it's not ideal."

"What we do is dangerous," White added. "Bike racing is

inherently dangerous, but the vast majority of drivers in team cars are experienced and very careful and are ex-bike riders themselves." Experienced enough to wait until the finish to collect discarded rain jackets, rather than collect them during the finale of a rain-soaked mountain stage, as White says the UCI commissaire directed.

DO YOU REMEMBER THE FIRST TIME?

By Marco Pastonesi, May 16 2021

Taco van der Horn and Tim Merlier's first stage wins. Victor Lafay's first win as a professional cyclist. Andrea de Marchi's first time in the pink jersey. Attila Valter: the first Hungarian to lead the Giro. The Giro is all about first times. Cyclists making their Grand Tour debuts, leading their teams for the first time, being baptised as conquerors and commanders. If the Tour de France seems more exclusively about established champions, the Giro has always seemed more open to the greats of the future, and to champions of one stage, one day, even if that's the only day they ever shine. It's a day of revelation.

The roads of Italy was where Fausto Coppi first made waves, in 1940, when he was just 20, and riding as a *gregario* to Gino Bartali. That's as if Raymond Poulidor had started out working for Jacques Anquetil, Luis Ocaña had been signed up as a domestique for Eddy Merckx, or Giuseppe Saronni had had to learn the ropes while saying "yes sir" to Francesco Moser. That only lasted as far as the stage from Firenze to Modena, when – helped by an issue with Bartali's bottom bracket, and given the go-ahead by team manager Eberardo Pavesi – Coppi revealed himself to the world.

Orio Vergani, who was following the race for *Il Corriere della Sera*, wrote, "I had seen Binda, Girardengo, Verwaecke and Bartali, all legendary champions. But on the climbs of the Abetone and Barigazzo I saw something new: an eagle, a swallow, I don't know what. Under the lashing rain and the drumming of the hailstones, his hands sat high and light on the bars, his knees turned implacably, his legs compensating perfectly on the hairpins as if they didn't know what fatigue was. He was flying, flying up those tough climbs. Coppi rode through a silent crowd, who didn't know who he was but just applauded and kept applauding."

Coppi wrote himself a place in cycling history, and Italian history. But there are those who enter the limelight only once, to achieve one single feat, to find glory between dawn and dusk and then fade away as the days pass. So it was that on the roads of the Giro Franco Magnani appeared like a shooting star. Today he's 83, lives in Cesena and pedals happily around on an electric bike. He only complains about the tiny degree of liberty he enjoyed, and how little it was, pulling painfully against the directions he was given by his team.

"I'd looked at the Mantua-Treviso stage, prepared for it, but it went wrong at the start. Just as the flag dropped, one of my team mates at Salvarani, Battista Babini, had a puncture. Out manager Luciano Pezzi told me to stop and wait for him. The group was heading up the road at 50 kilometres per hour, but I towed Babini back. A break of 15 had gone up the road in the meantime, so I got away from the bunch and caught them. That wasn't good enough for me, as I knew I wouldn't have a chance in a sprint, so I tried to get away several times, and escaped with Nelvio Vitali, who rode for Springoli.

"It was a two-up finish, with the others closing on us. I knew there was a dodgy corner at 300 to go, so I let Vitali lead into it – he went too fast, overshot the corner, and I went inside him. I had my arms in the air, but that evening at the dinner table, with the telly on, my team-mates didn't say a word. They had long faces. I was the only one watching the review of the stage, until Arnaldo Pambianco broke the silence: what's wrong with you? Didn't one of us win today?"

Even the first-timers get unforgettable experiences on the Giro, good and bad, joy and pain. I asked Pino Petito, who these days drives an ambulance in Civitavecchia, to tell me about going through heaven and hell. He opted for hell: the Gavia in the 1988 Giro. "We went up the climb from Ponte de Legno, hit the hairpins at Sant'Appollonia and the tragedy came just as we came out of the wooded bit. The road was nothing but mud and snow so we rode through the tracks left by the motorbikes. The rest was invisible: snow and mud, wind and ice and the torment of the freezing water. We all went up at our own speed, like men condemned to death. I had 41x23, and just rode blindly on what strength I had.

"At the top of the Gavia (2652m high) I had no idea where I was. The riders were getting into any vehicle they could find. I had legwarmers, armwarmers and a woolly hat. I began going down, carefully, afraid I would end up flying off into the abyss. A kilometre down the slope I was overtaken by Guido Bontempi and Paolo Rosola; they'd changed and warmed up and were descending like madmen. I saw a policeman, stopped and burst into tears. Halfway down, I got some whisky and drank half the bottle. Five or six kilometres from the finish I saw the Alfa-Lum team car with the heating full on and the fans blasting. I dropped my bike and got in, took five or six minutes to regain my faculties, then tried two or three times to get out, until finally I managed it. I was 143rd and last at the finish, along with three others: Longo, Zen and Cipollini – Cesare, Mario's brother. We were outside the time limit but they let us stay in the race."

The first Giro I covered for *La Gazzetta dello Sport* began when I had to wait for the riders at the airport in Groningen, because that year's Giro started from Holland. I was waiting for Michele Scarponi; I wanted to suggest that we worked on a race diary together, the diary of a *gregario*. He was working for Mario Cipollini. He said yes at once, and we had a crazy time writing about all his first times; getting on the podium, talking to television, and so on. On the rest day, for the newspaper, I asked Cipollini what he and his loyal servitors had done. "A 50 kilometre ride to keep the legs moving," he answered. Then for our diary, I asked Scarponi the same question. He replied that they had ridden to the first bar they could find, stopped for a coffee and a bit of a natter, then turned round and gone back to the hotel. That day, we both learned a lesson: mine was that you should never blindly believe what the bike riders tell you. His lesson was that you should always ask your boss to tell you the correct answer.

Marco Pastonesi spent 24 years as a writer on cycling at La Gazzetta dello Sport, *and has written numerous books on the sport.*

A GOLDEN AGE FOR BIKE RACING

By Peter Cossins, May 16 2021

The problem with golden ages is that we don't tend to know we've been in one until it's gone. This is an attempt to break that trend by declaring that cycling is now in the midst of a gilded era that will stand comparison with similar periods in the past, the post-war Coppi-Bartali-Bobet years, for instance, and the 1970s and 1980s when Merckx, Hinault, Fignon and LeMond were in their pomp. In fact, I'd suggest that it could surpass even those great epochs and assert that there's never been a better time to be a cycling fan.

There's been plenty of evidence of this in the Classics over the last couple of seasons, partly thanks to the emergence of a group of riders whose primary instinct is to attack rather than watch and wait. This kind of aggressive strategy is, of course, easier to employ in a one-day event where going full gas isn't going to have any repercussions the next day. Yet, the Grand Tours have also become much more engaging too as a spectacle, as the first week of this year's Giro d'Italia has underlined.

At the end of the race's second weekend, there have been great performances and talking points almost every day, beginning with Filippo Ganna's Turin time trial tour de force on day one, a performance of savage power and compelling beauty that it was impossible not to be wholly awed and impressed by, even if you're a TT agnostic like me.

Day two brought the first of three mesmerising bunch sprints, the kind of finishes that you should be watching from behind the sofa or through the gaps between your fingers as they're clamped over your eyes. Watching the coverage on French TV, I've lost count of the number of times that commentators Jacky Durand, Marion Rousse, Steve Chainel and Guillaume Di

Grazia have exclaimed, "*Ca frotte beaucoup. Oooh, la, la!*" as riders have bumped, barged and elbowed each other in the battle for position. Then there's that final explosion of speed, the action so frantic and rapid that you have to watch half a dozen replays before you can clearly see how the sprint unfolded.

One of the attractions of bunch sprints in the last few seasons, particularly at the Tour de France and Giro, is that there doesn't tend to be one dominating rider in the way there used to be when Mario Cipollini, Mark Cavendish and Marcel Kittel were in their pomp. Currently, there are usually at least half a dozen and even as many as 10 sprinters spread across different teams who are capable of winning if their teammates get the lead-out and positioning right, the momentum switching from one to another at each bunch finish.

In a similar way to the Vuelta a España and more so than the Tour, the Giro also tends to favour those riders whose principal hope of success is always likely to come in a breakaway. My highlight of the week was Taco van der Hoorn's solo victory in Canale on stage three. I suspect most fans were pedalling frantically with him, trying to give the gurning Dutchman an imaginary push as he gave all he had to hold off a peloton that somehow never get organised in its pursuit of the Intermarché-Wanty-Gobert rider. Then, as van der Hoorn approached the line, the gurn turned to the most wonderful grin when he realised that he'd done what he needed to and was about to win a stage at the Giro.

The victories taken by Joe Dombrowski at Sestola on day four, a long-awaited and much-deserved Grand Tour success for the American, by Gino Mäder at Ascoli Piceno two days later, the Swiss resisting the late charge by the big hitters, and by young Frenchman Victor Lafay at Termoli, were of the same type as Van der Hoorn's exploit. Each judged their effort faultlessly, their successes having a little more cachet because they took them when the peloton was still comparatively fresh and the stakes were high.

All the while, the overall contest has been bubbling very nicely, the favourites sparring occasionally with each other as first Ganna, then veteran Alessandro Di Marchi and, over the last three days, young Hungarian Attila Valter have savoured the prestige of wearing the *maglia rosa*. This "dosing" of the battle for the overall title is arguably the most significant change to Grand Tour racing over the last decade or so.

When I first started reporting on the sport in the early 1990s, the routes of the Grand Tours were forged using a very similar template: a time trial to begin with, a series of sprint stages, a longer time trial, then a big mountain test at the mid-point. This frequently resulted in the overall battle being all but finished when the race was only half-complete. The Tour became the most predictable of the trio of three-week stage races, the sport's biggest shop window reduced to a humdrum procession.

Over the last decade or so, the Grand Tour organisers have been much more canny when piecing together their routes, endeavouring to provide spectacle throughout while, at the same time, keeping the overall verdict in doubt for as long as possible. Messrs Prudhomme, Vegni and Guillén and their organising teams have become masterful at achieving this. Last year, for the first time, the winning margin at all three of the Grand Tours was less a minute. What's more, you have to go back to the 2016 Tour to find the last occasion when anyone finished a three-week race with a very comfortable margin, Chris Froome taking victory by four minutes and five seconds that year.

Today's stage provided another good example of a Grand Tour organiser serving up a route that delivered plenty to watch, but didn't kill the overall suspense. Egan Bernal's magnificent burst in the final few hundred metres on the gravel finish at Campo Felice that enabled him to claim his first GT stage win and *maglia rosa* may have installed him as favourite for the overall title, but the Colombian still has eight riders within a minute of him, and of them only Valter currently looks likely to drop out of contention quickly.

There's one more significant component to the upward trend in Grand Tours and indeed all racing at the top level, and this applies equally to women's events. The coverage is better than it has ever been, with a substantial improvement noticeable during the most recent seasons. The commentators and their expert consultants are more insightful, while the coverage is rarely dull, even on the most benign of sprint stages. Stats, interviews, historical interludes and analysis are all adding to a better viewing experience, their use complementing the wonderful images that have always made cycling such an attraction.

Going back to today's stage once again, all of these factors came together to produce four hours of fabulous entertainment. Clearly, not every Grand Tour stage and not every Grand Tour is going to be as consistently thrilling as this edition of the *corsa rosa* has been. However, the processions that were often the norm 10, 15 and 20 years ago are also far less likely to reoccur.

Over the past 30 years, racing has never been as consistently good as it is now. What's more, looking at the young talents already burning a trail through the sport – the likes of Tom Pidcock, Lorena Wiebes, Demi Vollering and Remco Evenepoel to name but four – this upward trend looks set to continue. This is an era to relish.

RED EYES IN THE WHITE DUST

By William Fotheringham, 19 May 2021

Jai Hindley's rainjacket in 2020, Remco Evenepoel's ear-piece in 2021. The moment in the penultimate sector of *sterrato* on the road to Montalcino, when the 21-year-old Belgian pulled the offending piece of plastic out of his ear will, I suspect, loom large in television montages of this year's Giro d'Italia, in the same way that Hindley's tortured attempts to get his jacket on at the top of the Stelvio did last year.

There had always been a question hanging over Evenepoel since his strong ride in the opening stage of the Giro in Turin: just how long could he live the dream? He had, after all, never raced over a week in his career and he had come to the Giro without any racing in his legs since August 2020 when he crashed into a ravine during the Tour of Lombardy. As a French commentator muttered while watching him struggle in Tuscany, "he wasn't born in Lourdes." Miracles don't happen, and if they do happen in cycling, eyebrows are raised.

The day before, during an assured, confident rest-day press conference, Evenepoel had been asked – inevitably – if he thought he could win the Giro. He wasn't going to answer that one beyond saying that if he didn't believe in himself he wouldn't be at the start. He also replied, later, that his legs had begun to hurt, and he hoped that it was the same for the other riders around him.

Montalcino was far from the first time Evenepoel had encountered adversity in his young cycling career. Merely to get to the Giro he'd had to recover from a broken pelvis, taking several months off the bike, and then he had had to deal with the fact that, late in the winter, recovery took longer than expected, meaning he couldn't race the start of the season. Starting the Giro in the shape he had done was remarkable in itself.

Having said this, this was adversity of a different kind. Evenepoel has hit trouble on the road before, cracking dramatically in the finale of the road race world championship in Yorkshire in 2019. But here he had started the day a whisker behind Egan Bernal, with whom he had been scrapping on equal terms, he was wearing a classification jersey and – in theory – he was the sole leader of the Deceuninck-Quickstep "wolfpack" after João Almeida had struggled earlier in the race.

This wasn't the Pack's finest hour. Normally they circle their prey in a cohesive unit, but in the Tuscan dust they looked more like Red Riding Hood's Grandmother than a big bad grey predator. They exhausted their energy in bringing Evenepoel back to the front after a rocky moment or two in the first portion of *sterrato*, meaning he had only Almeida for support. The Portuguese is leaving the team at the end of the season, and seemed in no hurry to rally round his young team-mate when he slid off the back in the penultimate section. Wolf-tails between legs.

If there was any comfort for Evenepoel, he wasn't the only team leader making a close acquaintance with the man with the hammer. Peter Sagan was an early casualty, as was Dan Martin. But *Mr Marteau* had a particularly busy time on the final draggy tarmacced climb, where EF Education First cruelly put the 15 riders in the lead group into the gutter, spitting them out one by one. To see Vincenzo Nibali shake his head and swing out of the line was one thing – the shark isn't that menacing these days – but it was quite another to watch Marc Soler or Giulio Ciccone give best after looking effervescent in the opening week.

At the pointy end, the Giro is increasingly becoming Bernal's race to lose; by the end of the dusty day he had only Alexandr Vlasov within a minute. Emmanuel Buchman shone on that final grovelling ascent, a reminder that in the not too distant past (2019) he had been tilting for the podium at the Tour de France. Hugh Carthy benefited massively from EF's strong collective showing, while Simon Yates and Damiano Caruso flew discreetly under the radar. Both remained well within reach without ever earning a mention in dispatches, which is the best way to be at this stage.

The biggest winner, along with Qhubeka-Assos's Mauro Schmid? The Giro. Televisually, this was sumptuous. It lacked the brutally dramatic images of 2010's mudfest, but, as Jørgen Leth said when shooting *A Sunday in Hell*, dust is visually more appealing than mud, and it offers the riders a better chance to race if they aren't slogging just to stay upright. The clouds of dust floated across the cypress avenues like gunpowder smoke on a battlefield, the riders floated in and out of focus like ghosts in fog, and the racing never relented for the final 70 kilometres.

And here's a final thought. Freddy Maertens once told me that after a dusty Roubaix, it took days to work the grit out of the eyes and lungs. There will be red eyes and sore chests on Thursday morning at the stage start in Siena, and the effects of this one day on the dirt roads to Montalcino may last – for some – as far as Milan.

REMEMBERING THE GIRO CLASS OF 2020

By Nick Bull, May 25 2021

They say a week is a long time in politics. I'm not sure what that makes the 214 days that have passed since Team Sunweb's Jai Hindley almost crashed near the top of the Stelvio removing his rain jacket and Egan Bernal's noticeably calmer and more controlled upper body strip approaching the finish line in Cortina d'Ampezzo on Monday. But the Colombian's return to Grand Tour form in this year's Giro d'Italia has overshadowed last year's break-out stars almost as quickly as their legends were born.

The reigning Giro champion, Tao Geoghegan Hart, opted against defending his crown in favour of targeting the GC at the Tour. Hindley, who was 15.7 kilometres away from winning the 2020 edition, came into the race declaring that he wanted to do "what I did last year – or maybe even better" but departed on Saturday with what his team described as a serious saddle sore. He was 25th overall at the time. "This is obviously not how I wanted my Giro to end," he said. "The team have really put in a lot to try and help, but the situation isn't improving and I really can't continue anymore."

Four more top-10 finishers in Milan last October also found themselves somewhere other than Turin a little over a fortnight ago while João Almeida, the *maglia rosa* for 15 days in 2020, crept back into the top 10 on Monday for the first time since stage three. Little wonder the two editions, separated by just seven months, feel very different.

Bernal's dominance in the opening two weeks reiterates that he's the second-best Grand Tour rider in the sport right now; combined with the large roadside crowds and a return to a May date this feels like a throwback to cycling in 2019. However, that should not diminish the achievements of Geoghegan Hart, Hindley et al. last year.

In the past decade, no rider has been as far off the race lead in terms of both position *and* time in a Grand Tour at the two-thirds mark as the Ineos rider was at last year's Giro (11th, at three minutes and 44 seconds). One cycling statistician calculated that Geoghegan Hart's, Hindley's and Wilco Kelderman's performance on the Piancavallo climb during last year's 15th stage was akin to riding a 38:15 on Alpe d'Huez, a time that has only been surpassed eight times, and by some questionable names at that.

Filippo Ganna was doing Filippo Ganna things and even Arnaud Démare's four stage victories, the first time that the Frenchman had ever claimed multiple wins in a Grand Tour, saw him replicate the likes of Bernard Hinault (1982), Eddy Merckx (1969, 1972) and Roger De Vlaeminck (1972, 1976). Démare's final win in that quartet, stage 11 into Rimini, may have seen him up against the likes of Álvaro José Hodeg, Simone Consonni, Rick Zabel and Nico Denz, but he still had to beat them. Ask Giacomo Nizzolo, he of 11 second-place finishes and no stage wins in the Giro fame prior to last Friday, how difficult claiming a victory in the race really is. "My goal was to be second," he joked after his long-awaited triumph in Verona. "Maybe that was the trick to gain the victory."

Grand Tour wins cannot be fluked. One factor that is understandably and rightfully overlooked when it comes to a certain American's success (sic) at the Tour de France is that the rider in question managed to avoid any serious crashes or performance-affecting sickness for seven consecutive years. It took Geraint Thomas nine Tour starts to finally have an unhampered run at the race, while Thibaut Pinot has abandoned three of the five editions he's started since finishing third in 2014.

The simplistic take on Thomas's Tour win three years ago is similar to saying that Carlos Sastre (in Alberto Contador's absence), Cadel Evans (benefitted from Leopard-Trek's indecisive joint leadership with the Schlecks) and Sir Bradley Wiggins (helped by the distance of the race's time trials) all won the Tours they should have won. We can remind ourselves of the perils that come with being the pre-race favourite at a Grand Tour; Simon Yates conceded over two-and-a-half minutes to Bernal on Monday. "The victory is a bit far away now," the Briton declared, having slipped to fifth overall.

Bernal's stage win on Monday came exactly 250 days after his Tour title defence ended with him abandoning the race last September. His nearest challenger going into Wednesday's summit finish at Sega di Ala is Bahrain-Victorious's Damiano Caruso. The Italian has never finished higher than eighth in his 13 Grand Tour starts, yet we're rightfully applauding Bernal's performance as opposed to critiquing the Colombian's opposition. We would do well to apply such an approach to Geoghegan Hart's victory. If, once the Londoner retires, his Giro win proves to be the highlight of his career, perhaps *then* fans and experts alike can make their assessments on the quality of that triumph. Hindsight remains an incredibly powerful evaluator.

Indeed, looking back, it's already striking how much Bernal downplayed his expectations going into the Giro. "Everything will depend on how my back responds. It's useless to make false promises," he said, sticking to Ineos' long-standing "day by day" PR line. Barring injury or illness, he's on course to win the race by the largest margin since Nairo Quintana in 2014. Then again, a week can be a long time in cycling, too.

WHEN THE LAST SHALL BE FIRST

By Marco Pastonesi, May 29 2021

Between sundown on the penultimate stage at Alpe di Motta and sunup on the final day when the Giro reaches Milan, the point at which this article is being written, translated and published, three Italians – Attilio Viviani, Matteo Moschetti and Riccardo Minali – seem destined to contest one particular award. Not the pink jersey, but the black, the one "given" to the last rider in the race – the equivalent of the Lanterne Rouge in the Tour de France.

The *maglia nera* is "virtual", and, in my humble opinion, also virtuous. To tell it straight, the *maglia nera* existed for a few years, but hasn't been around for a while. Now we have pink, lilac, white and blue, but not black. But everyone knows that the *maglia nera* is what the last rider in the overall classification wears, in spirit at least. It is nothing to be ashamed of, and it's definitely the case that Minali – who has an "advantage" of seven minutes on Moschetti and seven and a half on Viviani – will be happy to take it. It's better to come last than second or third-last, because the last man is in the history books.

The last men in the race give the first their status. Even Eddy Merckx was last sometimes. At the world championship in San Cristobal, Venezuela, in the Andes, in 1977; first in the professional road race, 255 kilometres in the rain was Francesco Moser, 33rd and last Eddy Merckx. But everyone knows that Merckx was the greatest, not on that day, but of all time. On that Sunday, September 4 1977, Merckx the Cannibal gave an extra edge to his hunger, gave extra value to that hunger, and lent an extra degree to his greatness even when he finished last. Ahead of Merckx was Raymond Poulidor, France's much loved *Poupou*, the eternal second who was in his usual place, but starting from the back.

Turning a result sheet, or better still an overall standing, upside down and looking at it back to front, has a certain purity to it. For everyone: rider, fan or journalist. It's a good way of mixing up the cards, letting in other points of view and re-evaluating your precedents and priorities. In Italy, and in Italian, the synonym for a *maglia nera* is Malabrocca. Luigi Malabrocca, a piedmontese from Tortona, and then flying the flag in the southern Swiss province of Ticino, a man who bred fish and was the Italian cyclo-cross champion.

When he understood that he couldn't match the great champions, Bartali and Coppi, he devised a new way of racing. He would escape behind the peloton, go into bars and never emerge again, he would hide in ravines, in hay-barns and in cellars. Once he hid in a well, a dry one, but a peasant lifted the cover off: "and what are you up to?" "I'm riding the Giro." Then he got back on his bike, went over the Passo Rolle, the Pordoi, Campolongo and Gardena – this was the mega stage through the Dolomites – and arrived at the finish last. Very much last. He was the blackest of black jerseys. It was the thing he did.

He did it because by finishing last in the standings, he would earn more money than all his fellow pros, apart from Bartali and Coppi. The *sportivi* – that's what they called the fans then, not *tifosi* – would all dip into their pockets to stump up something for him. Someone would modify a hat and turn it into a bag for alms, tips, pocket money. And with a bit of this and a bit of that, Malabrocca would cash in. Last in the 1946 Giro, even more last in the 1947 race, absent in 1948 and in 1949 he ran into a rider who was ruthless enough to finish behind him – Sante Carollo, a builder by trade from the Vicenza area. It was unthinkable: Carollo first (if you read the standings from the back), and second–the pity, the shame, the scandal of it! – Malabrocca.

Often the last man is the most honest. And very often, in a pure and ironic paradox, the last man is also the first: the first to suffer and slip off the back, the first to sit up and wave farewell to the bunch, the first to have a crisis and the first to abandon, the first to get into a team car or the broom wagon, the first to unpin his number and the first to pack his bags and go home. I have no shame: I'll always take the side of the guy who finishes last. The battle between the "favourite" Minali and his rivals Moschetti and Viviani raises my spirits, because the last man is the weakest, the most fragile, the most vulnerable. He's the most animal, vegetable, mineral. The most generous, solid and human. He's also the most stubborn when it comes to keeping going, keeping pushing. He's the most genuine, the most authentic, the truest. He's given up fighting against and among the others, he's been left to do battle with himself. And from that point onwards it's a matter of self-awareness, self-knowledge and self-motivation. It's a matter of faith.

Chapter Four: Mental Health, Equality, Racism and Getting Aero

IS E-RACING THE PATHWAY TO PARITY?

By Amy Jones, February 1 2021

This week saw the introduction of the 'Movistar Team Challenge'; four qualifying rounds of e-racing to whittle thousands of hopefuls down to just ten riders who will compete at the top level of virtual racing. Those who qualify will benefit from pro-level support from the likes of WorldTour nutritionists and coaches as well as receiving a bike, smart trainer and kit.

The Movistar Team Challenge is something of an inversion of what the Zwift Academy competition has set out to achieve for the past four years – using the platform to identify talent for the real-life Canyon//SRAM and Qhubeka Assos road teams – and marks a trend towards professional teams taking virtual racing seriously as a new discipline offering burgeoning potential for their sponsors.

Crucially, the Movistar E-team will be comprised of equal numbers of male and female riders – five of each – which is in keeping with a wider trend towards greater gender equality across e-racing.

In contrast to racing on the road, where decent prizes, fair salaries, and live coverage are a rarity, women who race in the virtual world tend to enjoy parity across the board. Of course this is, in part, down to the fact that there are no complicated logistics to organise, no need for vehicles, staff or other outgoings that make road racing an expensive endeavour, but it would have been just as easy for those in charge to default to the 'norm' and make the women's races shorter. Instead, the new discipline has harnessed the chance to make a change.

One of the main advantages that e-racing has on road racing in this sense is its financial model: IRL (in real life) women's races don't tend to make much money which hampers their ability to offer prize money and live TV coverage. Virtual platforms, however, turn profits from user's monthly memberships (Zwift was recently reported to be valued at over $1 billion) and benefit from free advertising as events are broadcast on platforms such as Eurosport.

In July 2020, with the world in lockdown, the virtual Tour de France presented an opportunity for the pro women to compete under the Tour de France name – something that is not currently an option on the road. The race, which took place on Zwift, offered equal distances and courses to the men, and all six stages were broadcast live on Eurosport and other major platforms.

For the first ever UCI eSports cycling world championships, which took place last December, also on Zwift, the prize money between male and female winners was equal, and, again, both the men and women raced over the same distance (50 km) on the same course with the race also broadcast live.

Winner of the women's title, Ashleigh Moolman Pasio, believes that e-racing presents an opportunity for female racers to experience equality that may transcend the virtual world and eventually influence the way real-life road racing events are conducted.

"ASO don't want to invest in women's cycling if it doesn't benefit them in the short term," she says. "But an event like the Virtual Tour de France forced them to – because Zwift said that they would only hold the event if it was equal for men and women and it was the best platform to hold the event on."

Moolman Pasio sees virtual racing as a way to make competing more accessible to those who may not have time to travel around to road races – particularly women who may have commitments such as childcare – by virtue of the fact that it's as easy as simply getting on a trainer in your own home. "I'm 35 but I still feel like I'm at the prime of my career, but I want to start a family so my career on the road is limited, but with e-sports my career is just getting started. I could have a baby and still race."

Of course, there are obstacles that make virtual racing on Zwift or other platforms difficult to access in other ways, namely that the cost of a smart trainer or power meter (in the region of between £400-£1,000+) and the subscription itself (£14/month for Zwift, £6.99 for competitor RGT) may prove prohibitive for some.

The fact remains, however, that the adaptability afforded to developers who can control their own virtual worlds on their respective platforms allows high-level virtual racing to achieve progress that real-life professional road racing has been struggling to reach for years.

**In July it was confirmed that Zwift will be title sponsors of the inaugural Tour de France Femmes in 2022.*

PINOT, DEIGNAN AND THOSE RULES

By Jeremy Whittle, February 10 2021

As a long-standing cyclist whose first fifty miles, many years ago, were ridden in trainers, T-shirt and football shorts, I've never had much time for The Rules, the self-styled diktat on achieving road cycling Nirvana through sock length, tan lines and sunglass design. These days though, as increasing numbers of riders struggle with the demands of the sport, it's Rule 5 that particularly jars: "Harden the fuck up." Rule 11 isn't much better: "Family does not come first."

Perhaps all the macho posturing is intended to be ironic, so haha, very funny etc. However, in all seriousness, the creaking reactions to the career traumas of several top riders in recent months haven't been too far removed from such archaic thinking. Yes, physically and mentally, cycling's a tough sport – probably the toughest of all – but you're not in the trenches, it's not war, nor is it a matter of life and death. This is nothing to do with being 'woke,' but about having perspective.

A few months ago, *La Course En Tete* pondered the apparent demise of Fabio Aru's career, after he quit the 2020 Tour de France in the Pyrenees, a decision which drew stinging criticism from his team management. A few years ago, it might have gone unnoticed, but in a watershed season characterised by uncertainty, growing debates over diversity and duty of care, and some truly worrying safety breaches, it seemed tone deaf.

The dehumanisation extends throughout the sport and would shame any other workplace. Recently, Lizzie Deignan bemoaned the negative reaction to her mid-career pregnancy. "I got to a position where I felt I almost had to apologise," Deignan said. "I don't think that a man in my sport would think he's betraying his team by starting a family." Thankfully then, for Deignan at least, family does come first.

Only a few days ago, Peter Cossins reflected on the issues that had had impacted on Tom Dumoulin's decision to pause his career. Now Thibaut Pinot, a rider who, to many, personifies the description 'mercurial,' has joined the ranks of those opening up about the brutal nature of their profession.

In a wide-ranging and engrossing interview with *L'Equipe* this week, Pinot spoke of his chronic self-doubt, about doping and his concerns over a "two-speed peloton," of the pressure of having a team built solely around him, his thoughts this winter of retirement, and of his love-hate relationship with the Tour de France.

Most stories that picked up on the interview focussed, perhaps understandably, on his comments on the "two-speed peloton," yet it was his revelatory remarks on his numerous crises in confidence that proved equally compelling. Admitting that he was in some ways 'unmanageable,' Pinot said that he sometimes didn't know how his coaches and sports directors had been able to carry on backing him. "If I was a team boss, I wouldn't want to have a guy like me on the team. I'd sell him, even give him away," he said with dry humour.

Adding that his brother Julien was the "only person" who really understood him, Pinot said that his 30th birthday, last May, had been a watershed moment, "not just in cycling, but in life generally." "It felt like the end of childhood to me," he said. "I think about how everything has evolved in cycling and in life in general and we're not going in the right direction. I think eventually I will be happy to quit cycling, because all of that will have gone too far."

Deignan meanwhile will continue to successfully align motherhood with her racing career. She has pulled that off with aplomb, particularly in a storming 2020, and will hope to continue her run of form into this Olympic year. She has always been a vociferous and direct spokesperson for women's cycling. "I've almost had to become an advocate for my sex, rather than just be a cyclist," she said.

On Thursday, the Tour de la Provence four day race starts in the south of France. Aru, now with the Qhubeka-Assos team, will be on the start line, no doubt hoping to rekindle his climbing form in the stage finish at Chalet Reynard ski station on Mont Ventoux. Pinot, who started his 2020 season at the race, has instead opted for the Tour du Haut Var, that's assuming his still delicate back does not hamper him.

For both of them, the past few months have been an acutely difficult time. Pinot's vulnerabilities, in particular, have often been on show. Both riders endured a torrid end to 2020, both riders experienced a crisis in confidence and contemplated retirement, and now, both riders are starting their 2021 season in the next few days.

So much for those so-called Rules.

BANNING AERO STYLES IS HISTORY REPEATING ITSELF

By William Fotheringham, February 17, 2021

Anyone who raced a quarter of a century ago would have smiled at the announcement from the UCI last week that they were going to ban professional riders from descending in the "super-tuck" sitting on the top tube position, and from using the "virtual tri-bars" position in which the rider drops their forearms onto the top of the bars and bungs their hands together as if in prayer.

In the early to mid-1990s, the Spinaci and Tiramisù bars produced by Cinelli and ITM were all the rage, well down into the amateur ranks. Little, simple extensions turned into mini jewels of design that clipped onto the bars (I was very upset never to get hold of a drilled out variant). The *modus operandi* in a race was pretty well set. You'd attack or move up the side of bunch on the drops of the bars, and the instant you were clear of "traffic", you whipped your hands onto the Spinacis, dropped forearms onto the top of the bars and you went aero. It was probably quicker, it definitely felt quicker, and your weight was, of course, safely supported.

It would have been pretty dumb to get into the Spinaci position when sitting tight on a wheel – although you could *in extremis* whip one hand across to the brake lever while keeping the other on the *Spinacus* – and I don't remember seeing anyone in the amateur races I rode doing that. I don't recall catching sight of any of the pro riders doing that either while watching the Classics and the Tour de France.

Nor do I recall seeing anyone crashing while actually using the aero position, although one thing was pretty obvious: you didn't want to hit a pothole with your hands out front – it never felt as if you could control the bike as safely as you could with hands on the brake levers or the drops, and bunny hopping felt like a no-no unless you were super confident or skilled. You could steer the bike while in the aero position, but it was a nuanced business. I liked my Spinacis, apart from one thing. They made the front end of the bike look very busy, at a time when floppy brake cables were only a recent memory and everyone was trying to get a sleek aero look to their bike. They didn't look as bad, however, as the Scott Drop-In bars that Greg LeMond pioneered in the early 90s. I've still got a pair of those lurking in my garage and they now remind me of a gate covered in candyfloss. Perhaps putting pink fluo bar tape on them was pushing the boundaries of taste a little bit too far.

There was general dismay when the UCI banned Spinacis and Tiramisùs, not least from Cinelli and ITM. (The Drop-Ins were dropped in 1992 I seem to recall.) The governing body's move came after a spate of massive crashes in the 1997 Tour de France. It was all about ensuring rider safety and reducing race speeds, we were told, although I wouldn't say, over the years, there was any reduction in either speed or pile-ups. I don't recall any evidence being presented around either argument. They were just banned. Full stop.

In fact, my hunch now would be that the Spinaci ban stemmed from the then UCI head, the late Hein Verbruggen's dislike of all things that smacked of progress and aerodynamics. This was the era when Verbruggen ran on to the track at a world championship to prevent Graeme Obree from riding in an unconventional aero position, and where the Hour Record was briefly, and bizarrely, set back to the Merckx era in a Luddite attempt to turn the aerodynamic clock back. I suspect that Uncle Hein simply didn't like the way Spinacis looked.

Which all makes me wonder about why I have no issue with the UCI banning sitting on the top tube or the "virtual" tribar position. To the best of my knowledge, neither position has caused a crash, certainly in the pro ranks. And I've happily raced using kit which has been banned on safety grounds, albeit with no more evidence in favour of a ban than in this latest case.

Then again, I've been terrified both in races and on training rides by amateurs adopting both the newly banned positions, though fortunately not at the same time. The ones that stick in the mind are a third cat road race where guys were sitting on the top tube on downhills that must have been all of 5% – *because they could* – and a training line-out down a very wet road with potholes and drain covers where one of our number insisted on constantly riding "virtual". *Because he could.*

As a race organiser, I've had discussions with commissaires about stopping amateur riders from sitting on the top tube: the officials weren't keen on them using the position either and would brief riders not to do it. But those riders could always argue – as did my acquaintance on that wet training ride – "*but the pros do it.*" With that defence gone, and no more TV images of the pros *doing it* – no matter how safely – the practices should die a death.

So I'm with Matteo Trentin on this one: whatever the moans from pros who will be inconvenienced – and possibly fined – in the short term, perhaps the UCI have actually got ahead of the game for once, and have scotched these practices before they become completely, dangerously, ubiquitous. The Spinacis were lost in a corner of my garage, and maybe the Supertuck and "going virtual aero" will end up in similar obscurity.

THE PRIZE MONEY PARADOX

By Amy Jones, March 8 2021

When at last the women's race season started at Omloop Het Nieuwsblad, discussion centered around how SD Worx (formerly, Boels Dolmans) had deployed their trademark team tactics to pull off yet another win. It wasn't long after the race, however, that the conversation took a different turn; to that of prize money. In the following days after the race the figures €900 and €16,000 bounced around cycling Twitter – boosted by a pie chart from the group Internationelles – held up to show that Anna van der Breggen's win was worth (in financial terms) 5% of Davide Ballerini's.

Such is the nature of online debate that a binary argument emerged, with one side advocating for equal prize money, no questions asked, and the other cautioning that there are much bigger fish to fry – namely live TV coverage.

Tomas van den Spiegel, the CEO of Flanders Classics – the group that owns the race – came to his organisation's defence saying he was "quite disappointed" with the backlash after "all the financial investments we have made into women's cycling for years now."

Van den Spiegel pointed to an equality-driven initiative from Flanders Classics dubbed *Closing the Gap* launched in early 2020, within which they have set several goals. They claim to be working towards full equality by 2023, including upgrading the level of one women's race each season (Omloop Het Nieuwsblad went from 1.1 in 2020 to 1.Pro in 2021) and equal prize money.

Elsewhere, many appeared to assert that instead of challenging inequalities we must instead celebrate – and be thankful for – incremental change as it comes. But while it is true that of course we should celebrate the wins and progress, applauding progress and campaigning for further change do not need to be mutually exclusive.

Lizzy Banks of Ceratizit-WNT told *cyclingnews.com* last Thursday: "The topic of prize money is a difficult one, and there is no magic answer, but it's a conversation that needs to be had and it's all part of creating an environment where women feel valued."

Ultimately, to treat this as an 'either-or' situation is to miss the overarching reality that in order to drive forward change people need to buy in, both ideologically and literally. How are we supposed to show investors, stakeholders and even would-be fans that women's cycling is worth just as much as the men's when figures like that show in real terms that it is not?

And what of the UCI's responsibility in this? In the wake of the debate and the stark visuals illustrating the discrepancy many were questioning why topping up the women's prize pot from the men's couldn't be the answer. It's a fair question, especially when the men are unlikely to miss it. The roadblock in this instance is none other than the governing body itself, who mandate a lower limit for prize money on men's WorldTour events. Ironically, for the last five years the UCI have themselves had equal prize money in their world title events, such as the recent world cyclo cross championships.

In the end, fans of women's cycling quite literally put their money where their mouths were after a GoFundMe was launched by Cem Tanyeri in an attempt to supplement the women's prize money ahead of Strade Bianche. The final total stood at around €22,000,surpassing the men's prize pot. Of course, the paradox of starting a GoFundMe to top up prize money is that – while it illustrates the appetite and support for women's cycling – it also removes responsibility from both the organisers and the UCI.

As the GoFundMe gathered traction, a new camp emerged; arguing that campaigning for more prize money only benefits a small portion of the upper echelons of the women's peloton who barely need it, and therefore doesn't advance the cause. Of course, by the same token, the men's peloton shouldn't need to be awarded prize money at all.

Ultimately, prize money probably isn't the hill to die on when it comes to pushing women's cycling forward, but rather something that will surely come organically off the back of more important structural changes such as increased live tv coverage and provisions for teams.

The response to the disparity has been an emotional one that speaks to the symbolism of such unequal prize funds rather than one that is rooted in practicalities. And that is fine, because what this debate has achieved is to highlight how far there is to go. In a round about way, it has actually united those with womens' cycling's best interests at heart reigniting debates around the inequalities and injustices that the women's peloton face. Parity is the collective end goal. The reality is, however, that there is more than one road to reach it.

CAMPAIGNING FOR CHANGE IN WOMEN'S RACING

By Sadhbh O'Shea, March 13, 2021

It is often said that consumer behaviour is what will force organisations and corporations to make change. In recent weeks fans of women's cycling have put their money where their mouth is with two fundraising campaigns. One aimed to ensure equal prize money at Strade Bianche and the other sought to get television coverage for the Healthy Ageing Tour. Both succeeded and showed a depth of passion that is often dismissed and continued a fine tradition of campaigning for progress within the sport.

Social progress for women has been inextricably linked with the history of the bicycle. It provided them with independence and even played a part in bringing to an end the practice of wearing hugely restrictive clothing such as corsets. Even now, in 2021, the bike continues to liberate women around the world.

In her 2011 thesis *Cycling and Women's Rights in the Suffrage Press*, Christine Neejer wrote that "cycling was an inherently political practice by many women activists in the 1890s" and it was "ultimately a meaningful and practical way [women] could challenge Victorian gender constructs and implement women's rights ideology in their everyday lives".

As long as there has been a bike, there have also been women racers defying the social preconceptions and going against the grain. In her book *Queens of Pain*, Isabel Best recounted some of those early rebels who defied sporting convention and set women's cycling on course towards what it is today.

In the late 1800s and early 1900s, trailblazers such as the Swede Tillie Anderson and Italian Alfonsina Strada showed that the idea women were physically incapable of sport was wildly wrong and set the stage for their successors. Progress would remain painfully slow and the first women's stage race, an idea that had existed for half a century for the men, did not come until 1955. In Britain, the first national road race championships did not happen until 1956. It was organised by the Women's Cycle Racing Association, which had been set up seven years earlier by British rider and official Eileen Gray. The rider from Bermondsey was a driving force for change in women's racing, beginning in the 1950s; women's world records were finally recognised during the late 50s and the UCI sanctioned the inaugural women's world road race championships, after years of pressure by Gray and other riders, in 1958. Nearly 30 years later, in her role as the president of British Cycling, Gray would also play a key role in a women's road race finally being included at the Olympic Games.

More recently, the Le Tour Entier movement, set up by Emma Pooley, Marianne Vos, Chrissie Wellington and Kathryn Bertine in 2013, has helped push the conversation around parity for women's cycling into the mainstream. It may not have achieved everything it wanted, although the return of a women's Tour de France seems so very close to becoming a reality, but their petition and the media conversation that ensued created the platform for the growth that has followed since.

The creation of the Cyclists' Alliance, led by Dutch former rider Iris Slappendel in 2017 was another major step for the sport. Despite the UCI neglecting to recognise the organisation, Slappendel and the rest of the team have held it to account and forced progress in a number of areas, including safeguarding and contracts.

As in those early days, progress has seemed slow at times but debates about gender equality in cycling are much more common place. People arguing on social media about how they think the sport will best grow might not seem like progress, but it is – open debate has led to two successful campaigns that have helped showcase women's racing and the strength of passion behind it.

Doors may be opening more easily but there are still many more to open before it's time to sit back and look upon what has been achieved. Women's racing must also look within itself for improvements. While the battle for gender equality is gaining speed, the fight for racial equality is one where the surface has barely been scratched. Meanwhile, parity for transgender women seems like a distant goal at this stage. If we want equality for women then it must be for all and not just some.

MOOD LIGHTING IN THE BUS AND THE GAP BETWEEN RHETORIC AND REALITY

By Jeremy Whittle, March 19 2021

Looking back, some of those early stories on what made Team Sky so special make for comical reading. "Team Sky's secret weapon is their team bus," read one article. "It gives us an edge," Bradley Wiggins said. "Team psychiatrist Dr Steve Peters has even overseen a mood-lighting system that he believes will enhance the riders' focus," gushed another story about the magical Team Sky bus. It may have enhanced their focus, yet it didn't help their eyes when it came to reading the labels on late-night Jiffy bags, but then maybe they had the mood lighting turned down very low when that mysterious delivery turned up at the 2011 Critérium du Dauphiné.

Richard Freeman, the former Team Sky and British Cycling doctor, has now lost his licence to practice medicine – subject to a possible appeal according to his lawyer – but the revelations may be far from over. Freeman now joins former Team Sky consultant, Geert Leinders, who was banned for life, in cycling's roll call of 'dodgy doctors.'

UK Anti-Doping, slow to react when first alerted to allegations and scepticism, now have their own credibility – and that of British sport – on the line, as they press further doping charges against Freeman, for "possession of prohibited substances and/or prohibited methods and tampering or attempted tampering with any part of doping control."

Meanwhile, British Cycling has stated that it found the verdict, "extremely disturbing," while Team Ineos, as the squad is now known, has said that "the team does not believe that any athlete ever used or sought to use … any performance enhancing substance. No evidence has been provided that this ever happened."

Part of the ennui some feel with the Freeman case, is not down to their world-weariness with doping in sport, nor with cycling's continuous struggle to ensure that its champions retain their integrity intact, but with the awful, nagging predictability of it all. In the late 2000's, as cycling battled to recover from the crippling aftermath of the Festina, Pantani, Puerto and Armstrong scandals, it was all going to be so different – Dave Brailsford, the performance guru behind that windfall of Olympic gold medals, had assured us all that Team Sky would be. When Team Sky launched, there was a stampede to get on board the gravy train. Cycling in Britain had never had it so good.

We'd had the Danish gold rush at the Tour de France with Bjarne Riis, the German gold rush with Jan Ullrich and of course the Stateside gold rush with Lance Armstrong. Now it was the turn of the Brits to take road racing by storm. Yes, you could win the Tour, and if you had deep pockets and mood lighting, you could win it clean. All we had to do was believe.

Suddenly, cycling was cool in Britain, and it was mainstream. The years of being laughed at, mocked and derided, were over. Now, as the London Olympics and a Yorkshire Grand Départ loomed large, there was money to be made. Suddenly every banker, restaurateur and hedge fund manager had clambered out of their BMW, pulled on some Rapha kit and bought a Pinarello.

Ex-riders from the skinflint Premier Calendar, who'd spent their careers living in bungalows in Barnsley, driving to races in beaten-up Citroëns, crossing swords in city centre crits with Shane Sutton, might look for a well-paid back-room job working for Team Sky. And at last, young British talent could see a clear route to the top. Now they could dream of living in Monaco and training on the Cote d'Azur, riding with F1 superstars and driving Maseratis and Jags.

But in the effort to make cycling cool, while winning races, keeping the gravy train on the tracks and the sponsorships lucrative, idealism and innocence slipped away. The lessons of Riis, Ullrich, and Armstrong were quickly forgotten. Hubris took over, the gravy train became a runaway express, and as the successes grew in number, so did the scepticism.

At the root of it all was the pursuit of serial success, wealth and fame, a characteristic shared with previous cases, where riders were welcomed onto chat shows, courted by ghost writers and treated like rock stars. "Brad wants to be famous in England," former team mate David Millar said once of Wiggins's move to Team Sky. "He wants more. He wants to be able to mingle with pop stars, be treated as a pop star."

If you were one of those that questioned Team Sky, you would be shouted down, and called out as 'unpatriotic,' particularly in the build-up to, and aftermath of, the 2012 London Olympics. The naiveté of an enthused home audience, new to cycling and unschooled in the inner workings of the peloton, ensured that few were interested in really stepping back and taking stock.

As a journalist, if you asked questions, you were dismissed, or at times, subjected to heated phone calls. You got fobbed off, sent around the houses, pursuing wild goose chases. It was a time-buying tactic, reliant on the journalist running out of energy, budget or inclination, and based on the expectation that the narrative would quickly move on to more positive angles. It usually did.

There was initially little real appetite in the mainstream media to question Team Sky, British Cycling or Dave Brailsford, not until the Jiffy bag story broke. Of course, there had been a steady drip drip of other stories – the failure of zero tolerance, the relationship with Geert Leinders, the use of Tramadol, the confusion over Froome's and Wiggins' TUEs, the controversy over Froome's salbutamol case – but now all of those have been superseded by the dramatic outcome of the Freeman hearings.

At the end of a week of Sky-bashing, in which ex-rider Jonathan Tiernan-Locke mocked Team Sky's claims of zero tolerance in a coruscating interview on *cyclingnews.com,* the truth of what really went on remains unclear. Is this all a storm in a teacup, or merely the tip of the iceberg? And then what does competing 'clean' really mean? It would appear to mean different things to different people. Is tinkering with TUE's clean? Tactical use of Tramadol? Certainly to the minds of most who bought into the Team Sky mantra of marginal gains, it won't have included medical advisers like Leinders and Freeman, nor unexplained and untraceable batches of testosterone-related products.

Brailsford has not yet publicly responded to the outcome of the Freeman hearings and nor has Ineos Grenadiers patron, Jim Ratcliffe, who stated when taking over the team that any proof of wrongdoing would end the relationship. Flurries of tweets and pledges of support from riders and staff have buoyed Brailsford through previous crises. Not this time, it seems.

In the end in these affairs, it always seems to come down to who you choose to believe and who most deserves your trust, your faith. Right now, with Freeman struck off and portrayed as a lone wolf, that's a hard question to answer.

But just remember, as you try to make sense of the history of Team Sky, what we were all asked to buy into when this saga started a decade or so ago: it was transparency and professionalism, accountability and propriety – and the mood lighting on the team bus – not dodgy doctors, Jiffy bags, TUEs, or Tramadol.

BIDONS, LITTER, LONG SOCKS: ARE THEY THE KEY ISSUES?

By Jeremy Whittle, April 7, 2021

In the aftermath of the littering incidents that led to disqualifications and debate in the past few days, there has been much discussion about the draconian nature of these new UCI rules, and of how ruthlessly they have been implemented. If you are Kyle Murphy, Letizia Borghesi or Michael Schär, all of whom were disqualified and fined under the UCI's new littering rule, you might feel harshly treated. At the same time, the world governing body are responding to growing concerns over cycling's eco footprint. Pressure is growing to ensure there is no disconnect between the greenest machine – the beautiful, wondrous bicycle – and the gas-guzzling bubble, tossing its detritus into the countryside, that accompanies all major races.

Last September, there was open derision in France towards the Tour de France's lack of green credentials, with several cities and regions making their feelings plain. The Tour, cycling's flagship race, was described as "macho and polluting," by Gregory Doucet, mayor of Lyon. Other city mayors weighed in too and called for greater environmental awareness within cycling.

The need to respond to those expectations fits with the vision that current UCI President David Lappartient set in place when he was first elected. Greener, cleaner, and more inclusive, cycling under Lappartient would become more modern and reflect the values and sensitivities – both ethical and political – of a younger and more diverse audience. Were those mayors really calling for action on *bidons* and gel wrappers, or as many think more likely, throwing their hands up in horror at the bigger picture: the proliferation of luxury buses, team vehicles, guest cars, media vans, TV helicopters and short haul flights, ferrying the entourage back and forth across Europe.

In fairness, the 'autumn' Tour of September 2020 was a far smaller event, with a reduced footprint. Travel restrictions imposed by the pandemic forced change and Racing in the Time of Covid generally proved more eco-friendly than in the past. Transfers for example, were usually executed by bus, rather than by air.

At the same time, it's increasingly apparent that the UCI under Lappartient is at a crossroads. The governing body can tinker with their sport – gel wrappers, sock length, descending positions – or they can be progressive and actively promote real and lasting change, on sportswashing, racism, gender equality and environmental impact.

When he stood for Presidential election, Lappartient's manifesto cited these key goals: Strengthening the authority of the UCI with a President ensuring real and effective leadership – Placing the UCI at the service of National Federations – Making cycling a sport of the 21st century – Developing an ambitious vision for professional cycling – Ensuring credibility of sporting results and protecting athletes.

Those objectives – let's call them KPIs or key performance indicators – have a somewhat vague air. What does 'making cycling a sport of the 21st century' really mean in practical terms? What exactly is his 'ambitious vision'? Where are the specific and measurable objectives for his goals?

While all this has been going on, a rider whose biggest fault is his occasionally reckless and impetuous sprinting has this week been forced out of a major race due to the mental anguish of serial racial abuse. There has been a trickle of support for Nacer Bouhanni, but like most athletes who have been victims of racial abuse, those in positions of power and influence have sat on their hands.

On Wednesday, Bouhanni, exhausted from fending off the largely racially motivated attacks of trolls on social media, withdrew from the GP Scheldeprijs. Ironically, this came as the UCI belatedly posted a statement condemning the abuse he had received. The Frenchman had raced on Sunday at Roue Tourangelle, but admitted he had come close to pulling out of that race also. "I told the team manager that I couldn't do it anymore, that psychologically I couldn't go," he said, later adding: "It feels like no one is listening to me, that no one understands me."

You might reasonably think that 'Making cycling a sport of the 21st century' would include exiling racism from the sport you governed and that such an issue would, by some distance, have precedence over dropped gels and bidons. And, after the events of the past few days, you might also ask, what is the UCI really for? Disqualifying riders for accidental littering, or rejecting discrimination and hate? What is the biggest challenge for international cycling? Greater diversity or discarded *bidons*?

To many working in cycling, the UCI need to achieve clarity on what really matters, on how they can promote and achieve a genuine and healthy growth of cycling's appeal. Yet they seem confused. For example, the governing body will point, as will other champions of diversity, to the Tour of Rwanda as a shining example of the sport's multi-racial appeal. But there is a significant problem here, too, one that the UCI seems unable or unwilling to acknowledge. The Tour of Rwanda is widely seen as a sports-washing event, supported by a President whose 'democracy' has been criticised in the international media and by Amnesty International. "Dictators such as Kagame – and those who show a repeated disdain for human rights and the rule of law in practice – do not deserve the plaudits or the financial support that they often receive," the *Washington Post* wrote in a September 2020 report. However, in 2019, UCI President Lappartient travelled to Rwanda to start the first stage of the race. Maybe he doesn't read the *Post*. Or maybe the UCI needs to work on its due diligence. At the same time, Rome wasn't built in a day. Neither the UCI nor ASO can change a century old sport overnight. But they could certainly do better.

They could publish, in collaboration, a coherent three year plan that sets out specific and measurable KPIs, on eco footprint, on diversity of race and gender, on ethical practice and appropriate relationships, against which they and their stakeholders can measure their performance. That then, might be something that the lifelong cycling fans, many of whom are intellectually and emotionally so invested in the sport, could at last really get behind.

IN PRAISE OF THE DAUPHINÉ

By Peter Cossins, June 9 2021

I've always had a soft spot for the Critérium du Dauphiné, a race that rarely concerns itself with having a prelude to the mountains, usually opting to direct those taking part towards short and steep hills from the off, then steadily lengthening the extent of the climbing over each consecutive stage. It eventually reaches a final day when the riders predict "all kinds of chaos" and that "anything could happen" because no one team has got the energy to impose any kind of control. This year's edition followed this template precisely – well, until the last day, that is.

Since 2016, the race has ranged well beyond the Dauphiné region in an ever-widening search for towns willing to pay to host its starts and finishes. In 2019, this was officialised with the introduction of the sub-title "Auvergne-Rhône-Alpes", which has resulted in the early stages taking place in the rolls and ravines of the Massif Central rather than the foothills of the Alps. Purists may not like this development, but it's enabled the race to survive and it hasn't affected the spectacle a jot.

The first couple of stages illustrated this perfectly. On the opening day, second-year Belgian pro Brent van Moer announced himself to his peers and the rest of the cycling world with a solo performance of staggering power and panache. The last surviving member of the escape group, the Lotto Soudal youngster held off a very fast-moving bunch to win on a tough finishing circuit in Issoire.

Day two ran to a similar pattern, with Bora's Lukas Pöstlberger playing the van Moer role to perfection as he held off the bunch on the tough final climb, then descended like a demon into the finish at Saugues, where Sonny Colbrelli was runner-up for the second day in a row. Mention should also be made of the beautiful terrain in and around the Allier river valley, which provided a magnificent reminder that France can still surprise even the most seasoned race-goer.

On day three, Colbrelli, described by B&B Hotels climber Pierre Rolland as being "*fort comme une vache*", or as strong as an ox, lived up to that billing by barrelling away from his rivals up the sharp drag into Saint-Haon-le-Vieux to take the stage win that always seemed to be coming. Just as memorable, though, was the sight of Fabio Jakobsen battling for position in the final kilometres as he contested his first bunch sprint since that awful crash in Poland last year. Although the Dutchman didn't have the legs to sustain his effort in the final kilometre, he looked radiant at the finish having felt the buzz of adrenalin that a bunch gallop always brings.

I'm not usually keen on a time trial, but the Dauphiné's test between Firminy and Roche-la-Molière was thrilling because it was so unpredictable. I can't remember who it was that said at the finish that they weren't sure what kind of rider it suited (Richie Porte?), as the 16.4km test where there was never any more than 400m of straight road before the next bend, descent or, towards the finish, sharp ramp defied almost everyone's attempt to get the pacing right.

No one was caught out more obviously by it than Geraint Thomas, the quickest by seven seconds at the first checkpoint, but only good enough for 10th on the line, a place behind Pöstlberger, who lay flat out on the road for some time after a courageous ride that enabled him to retain the lead by one second. Thomas responded the very next day, though, attacking on the exit of a close to 360-degree corner a kilometre from the line in Saint-Vallier and then just resisting the ox-like Colbrelli's final burst of power and speed.

The first stage produced that rarest of things, a day when

Movistar's riders collaborated perfectly and out-thought their rivals to set up Alejandro Valverde for his first stage win at the race since 2008. This augured well for the final weekend, pitching the Spanish team against Ineos, with Astana, AG2R and Bora very much in the contest too with two contenders each.

The first and toughest of the final two stages took the race to La Plagne, once a regular feature on the Tour de France route but not visited since 2002. The return was memorable, firstly for Mark Padun's completely unexpected victory, the Ukrainian jack-hammering the pedals as if on a butcher's bike but with very impressive effect. Behind him, the battle between the GC contenders was drawn-out, engrossing and eventually concluded with Richie Porte emerging as the strongest. He'd only been in the leader's yellow and blue jersey for a few minutes when he was being reminded by the press of his fate in 2017, when he led into the Dauphiné's final day only to be harried, ambushed and almost broken by defeat right at the last.

"Expect chaos" was the GC contenders' forecast for the concluding stage to Les Gets. Instead, it delivered what was close to a rerun of the La Plagne stage, Padun winning again, this time from the breakaway, and Porte relatively untroubled as Ineos controlled his rivals perfectly. Thirty-six years on from the only previous victory by an Australian in the Dauphiné, Phil Anderson's 1985 success, 36-year-old Porte claimed what had hitherto been an elusive title.

Looking ahead to the Tour, the Dauphiné suggested that Ineos will be the team to beat. Victorious at Catalunya, Romandie, the Giro and the Dauphiné, their meltdown in this race last year now looks like an aberration. Thomas is a genuine Tour contender again, while Porte and Tao Geoghegan Hart look unflappably strong. Astana, Movistar, Bora, AG2R and Bahrain will be buoyed by their performances too.

On the other hand, UAE Team Emirates' hopes of helping Tadej

Pogačar defend the Tour title took a knock. In the Slovenian's absence, Brandon McNulty slumped, apparently affected by his return from training at altitude in the US, and the rest of the team were anonymous. Jumbo-Visma, who were also missing their Slovenian talisman in Primož Roglič, also struggled, Steven Kruiswijk their highest finisher in 15th place. Both of these teams will have to improve significantly if they want to match Ineos.

But the final word should go to the Dauphiné, which once again served up a week of enthralling racing, mostly free of the shackles that will come on at the Tour. For that it should truly be cherished.

Chapter Five: The Rise of Pog and the Return of Cav

TOUR DE FRANCE TIME LINE

June 13: Ineos dominate the Tour build-up, with Richard Carapaz taking the Tour of Switzerland after Richie Porte wins the Critérium du Dauphiné

June 26: Julian Alaphilippe wins at Landerneau in the rainbow jersey; Demi Vollering takes the final edition of La Course by Le Tour de France

June 27: Mathieu van der Poel takes yellow at Mûr de Bretagne, referencing his grandfather Raymond Poulidor who never wore the *maillot jaune*

June 28: a mass pile up mars the run in to the finish at Pontivy with Primož Roglič badly cut up; he will abandon a few days later

June 29: at Fougères, Mark Cavendish takes the first of four stage wins

July 3: at Le Grand Bornand, Tadej Pogačar pulls on the yellow jersey after crushing the field on the final climb

July 9: Cavendish draws level with Eddy Merckx's record tally of 34 Tour stage wins

July 18: Wout van Aert clinches a hat-trick of stage wins, mountain, time trial and sprint, by outpacing Cavendish on the Champs Elysées after winning the previous day's time trial at Libourne. Pogačar takes his second overall victory in two years, from Jonas Vingegaard and Carapaz. Cavendish takes green, Pogačar the KOM.

STRAINING THE CIRCUIT BOARD

By William Fotheringham, June 25 2021

On paper, looking ahead to the Tour de France should be simple. Look at the route, assess the field, figure out whose results trajectory looks good. Maybe some boffin will one day invent a computer programme that does it through an algorithm. Perhaps Sir Dave Brailsford has got one already. In fact, I'm sure he has. Because between 2012 and 2019 (with due respect to Vincenzo Nibali who bucked the trend in 2014) it was pretty simple: a rider in a Team Sky or Ineos jersey would win.

This year, the computer's circuit boards would be straining a bit. The algorithm didn't really work out in 2020, and I'm not sure it would be any simpler in 2021, because however you look at the next three weeks of bike racing, none of it is straightforward. There are five big favourites for the Tour, as I read it, and each of them has a questionmark attached. Tadej Pogačar, Geraint Thomas, Richard Carapaz, Primož Roglič, Miguel-Angel Lopez: each comes with a caveat.

Pogačar starts as the big favourite, because he looks the most complete in every area, because the route doesn't seem to present any real dangerpoints for him, he's had a perfect build-up, and because he's strengthened his team, which was the one achilles heel he had in 2020. Now for the caveat: he's not the surprise any more, so there will be no more flying under the radar. And I wonder how that team will function in adversity – you often find when the leader is flying so are the team mates, but it's how they gel when something goes wrong, as it will at some point.

Thomas and Carapaz can be dealt with together, as you imagine they will be for much of the next three weeks. They are complementary – Carapaz stronger in the high altitude finishes,

Thomas better in the time trials – and they have the might of the Ineos *Galácticos* behind them, led by Richie Porte and Tao Geoghegan Hart, both of whom are qualified to lead the team as well. You'd imagine that the Ineos leadership question won't be resolved at least until the Ventoux, the first really massive climbing test, and I just wonder if Carapaz will edge it. The questionmarks? I can't see Thomas climbing at the same level as Pogaçar, plus I wonder about Thomas's age, and I can't see Carapaz in the same time trialling bracket as Pogačar or Roglič. Roglič has the benefit of last year's learning experience plus the support of a climbing unit that is almost as good as Ineos, and he is Jumbo's uncontested leader. He has grit to burn and we know he can time trial on his day, if you look at last year's Vuelta as well as the Tour. His form is impossible to read as he hasn't raced since April, so either he's supremely confident or he's taking a massive risk. I can see him racing strongly for 90 per cent of the Tour, then cracking somewhere like Pla d'Adet or Luz Ardiden.

Lopez can climb well, we know he can win a meaty stage race, and if Movistar get behind him they are a formidable unit. But the time trial questions remain, and of the five he's probably most vulnerable if the race hits cross winds, because 2021's Movistar doesn't have a Tony Martin or a Luke Rowe. Briefly, I'd add in two other names, for the podium if not the final win: Rigoberto Urán and Julian Alaphilippe. Urán for the day-to-day consistency he can show, Alaphilippe for his ability to make things happen.

There's one element to the Tour that you can never afford to ignore, another area where that algorithm might struggle: the unknown. It remains cycling's greatest attraction, and the Tour's. To go a bit Rumsfeldian, it's the fact that you know stuff is bound to happen, but you can't have any idea what or when. To start with, the crashes: at almost any moment, but especially in the first week, all predictions can be rendered void in an instant. Then, the wacky stuff like Julian Alaphilippe taking a bottle at the wrong moment, or Pogačar's team going missing just as the race splits in a crosswind, both among 2020's curious moments. The Tour is 21 days of chaos theory. Think back to 2012: how would that race have been different if Chris Froome had not gone into a pothole on the Liège stage? 2014? The cobbled stage where Vincenzo Nibali won the Tour in the first week. It's fashionable to pan the Team Sky years as being predictable, but the fact is that Chris Froome won his Tours in some fairly unlikely ways – running up Mont Ventoux, attacking downhill in the Pyrenees, blowing everyone away in a crosswind in the *midi*.

As Tours go, 2020 was even more random than most, thanks to the pandemic; 2021 may look as if it's back to business as usual, but as Henri Desgrange realised back in 1903, if you put a load of cyclists on the road, and send them off around France, you end up with an enthralling mix of sport and soap opera. One thing is certain: the opening weekend in Brittany is set to be one of the hardest ever, and all those who get to Mûr de Bretagne on Sunday within reach of the leaders will breathe a sigh of relief.

Seven questions for the next three weeks

Can Tadej Pogaçar kick on? Answer: yes. Winning a first Tour de France is never easy, but winning a second is so hard that it moves a rider onto another level. The bulk of Tour winners manage it only once. But "Pog" has looked so good this year, posting an astonishingly high hit rate in the races he's started, that it's perfectly possible to envisage him building on his success of 2020.

Will the Ineos trident be Movistar mark two? Answer: maybe. In theory, having three definite leaders – Thomas, Carapaz and

Geogheghan Hart – plus a wild card in Richie Porte is a huge advantage. Given Pogaçar's form so far this year, and the usual uncertainties of the Tour, it is far better to be taking him on in numbers, and the Ineos management have recently coped well with multiple leaders. But it will only work if at least two of the trident are as good as "Pog" and "Rog" when the chips are down. If it starts to go wrong and egos get bruised… well, it all gets very interesting.

Who will turn up from left field? No clear answer to this, because the nature of modern cycling means that riders and teams turn up at Grand Tours without clearly posting their form. Not many would expected Sunweb to win three stages at last year's Tour, or Qhubeka to land three at this year's Giro. Given the freak nature of last year's race in terms of timing and run-in, this year's race looks more like business as usual. There's not as much space for unproven talents, but the ones I will be looking out for are Bruno Armirail, Stefan Bissegger, Jonas Vingegaard and Mark Donovan.

What effect will the time trial stages have? The constant tinkering with the format in recent years means the last time there were two time trials was 2017 – and the first was a relatively short one at 14km – and the last time there were two time trials of comparative length at similar points in the race was 2008. In 2017, the Marseille time trial on the penultimate day seemed to make for conservative riding in the Alpine stages immediately beforehand. My hunch, this year, is that the first time trial won't eliminate many contenders, and the second will merely confirm the verdict of five extremely hard days in the Pyrenees. But I might not put my mortgage on it…

Will the pressure get to Julian Alaphilippe? No. Who would be a French star trying to perform in the home Tour? Remember what it did to Thibaut Pinot in 2015 – not nice. My sense is that by his nature Alaphilippe is not a GC rider, but a rider more in the Classics register who can knock out a good GC ride on occasion. That might seem a weird thing to say of a rider who led the race for 14 days and finished fifth overall in 2019, but he said today that he sometimes forgets exactly where he ended up overall that year. What that means is that, as he's not worrying if he's seventh overall or ninth, Alaphilippe can switch off on certain days and focus on what he does best, and that's a vital safety valve.

Will Mark Cavendish win a stage? Yes. For sure, he's 36, and for sure he insists he hasn't prepared specifically. But behind Caleb Ewan this isn't the strongest sprint line-up I've seen at the Tour, with no Dylan Groenewegen, no Pascal Ackermann, and (obviously) no Sam Bennett. Yes, Wout van Aert and Mathieu van der Poel will get in there occasionally to mix it up, but Cavendish has the best sprint train in front of him, arguably the best lead-out man in Michael Mørkøv and he has six chances before the race reaches the Pyrenees. Ewan should win at least two stages of the eight on offer before Paris, but the random nature of sprinting means there will be openings.

Which is the one unmissable stage? The double ascent of Mont Ventoux in the second week. It's a unique prospect and it falls at just the right time to set up the overall battle for the rest of the race.

MARK CAVENDISH: AN A TO Z

By William Fotheringham, July 1 2021

***A is for Age.* He's 36. Most sprinters are in carpet slippers by this stage. It's also for Academy (Great Britain) which is where he came to prominence back in the dark days when Lance Armstrong won the Tour every year, when jerseys were flappy and before disc brakes were seen on road bikes. Also for Alaphilippe, Julian, who isn't above putting in a big turn at the front to help his Manx team mate win.**

B is for Bank. Cav worked in one on the Isle of Man in his early amateur days saving money to go and race in Belgium. It gave rise to my favourite Cav quote, of his coach Rod (see E) Ellingworth: "He turned me from a fat banker into a world champion." Also for Ballroom Dancing, which he did way, way back in the day. Also for Bennett, Sam, DQS first choice sprinter for the Tour, sidelined with Knee. Therefore probably also for Bloody Hell.

C is for Châteauroux obviously. Also for Copenhagen, where he won the World's. Also for Champs Elysées. Will Cav get there in 2021? Finally: Comeback.

D is for Deceuninck-Quickstep. The best lead-out train in the world, which has led a bevy of top sprinters to Tour success. Also for Declercq, Tim, who puts in the hard yards at the front of the bunch for more kilometres than any of us care to count.

E is for Ellingworth. Cav's first coach, a definitive influence back in the day. Also Epstein Barr, the virus that laid Cav low in 2017-18.

F is for Ferry. Cav spent a lot of time on it travelling from the Island to the mainland as an amateur; it was character-building, he says.

G is for Green. Can he hold it to Paris and win it for a second time. Also for *Gruppetto.* That's where he will be until Tuesday next week, when it's the next (possible) sprint stage. Also for Generations of sprinters: Cav has proven faster than several over the years. And Greipel, André: a rare contemporary from the early days who is still racing.

H is for Holm, Brian, another defining influence: they have been working together since Cav's earliest years as a pro, and when he won the World's in 2011, Holm was the man Cav wanted in the team car with Rod Ellingworth. Also for HTC-Columbia, where Cav won the bulk of his Tour stages.

I is for Island. The Isle of Man. You can take Cav out of it, but you can't take it out of Cav.

J is for Jersey. Not the island. The full set of *maillots distinctifs* on the Cav wall: points and leaders from all three Grand Tours, plus the rainbow from 2011.

K is for Knee. Sam Bennett's. One man's bad fortune is another's windfall. One racer's patellar pain is another's pumping victory salute.

L is for Leadout men. Mark Renshaw in the HTC years. Michael Mørkøv now. Sir Bradley Wiggins famously at Team Sky, up the Champs Elysées, yellow leading out rainbow jersey. Bernie Eisel, with whom he spent 470 race days (thanks *procyclingstats.com* for that one) and now Julian Alaphilippe. It's also for Luck. You make your own.

M is for... He who shall not be named. Also Martin, Tony, a team mate back in 2008.

N is for numbers. He's won 32 stages in the Tour. He's won 7 times this year. He's won more Grand Tour stages than anyone except Merckx (sssshhh don't say the name) and Mario Cipollini.

O is for Olympics, a bit of a bugbear because in 2008 he quit the Tour early to race in Beijing and it went wrong and in 2012 the London road race didn't work out. Silver in the omnium in 2016 in Rio filled the gap. Also Opposition: this year, Bouhanni, Philipsen, Merlier, Bol, Sagan.

P is for Patrick Lefevere, the DQS manager who hired Cav back in 2015, and then again, in extremis, this year. Also for Peta Todd, Cav's other half.

R is for Romantic. In an attempt to play down the idea of winning in Châteauroux, Cav dismissed the notion as "romantic". He was right not to hype up his chances, but how else can you describe the feat of winning three Tour stages in the same town in 13 years, with one of those wins your first victory on Tour? That's pretty damn romantic in my book. R is also for Record and Retirement but we don't mention either of those.

S is for San Remo: 2011. Also for Sprint Stages. There are a potential eight in this year's Tour, of which we have had three.

T is for T-Mobile. Cav turned pro for them in 2007 and rode his first Tour in their iconic pink jersey, which got a little ripped at times. Other Teams: High Road (2008), Columbia-HTC (2009-2011), Team Sky (2012), Quickstep (2013-15), Dimension Data (2016-19), Bahrain (2020): And for Tears; after all he's been through, who wouldn't shed a few? Also Triple: in 2011 he won stages in all three Grand Tours.

U is for Unthinkable. Last autumn, that is how you would have described the current scenario of Cavendish riding for Deceuninck-Quickstep and being six days into the Tour, wearing the green jersey with two stage wins under his belt.

V is for Victory salute. 153 of them and all different.

W is for World (road race) Championship: 2011.

Y is for yellow. Cavendish's win at Omaha Beach in the 2016 Tour put him in the *maillot jaune*, completing the full set of wearing leader's and points jerseys in all three Grand Tours. It also prompted team-mate Steve Cummings to be seen at the front of the bunch the following day, which was pretty remarkable too on a flat stage.

Z is for Zabel. For trivia fans: when Cavendish won in Chatearoux in 2008, in third place was Erik Zabel, who dominated sprints between 1994 and 2001. When he won in Châteauroux in 2021, Erik's son Rik (born in 1993) finished 14th.

TIME TO STOP CALLING FOR BLOOD

By Sophie Smith, July 5 2021

Our great sport really doesn't help itself sometimes. The peloton is battered, bruised and missing some of its biggest names after only the first week of the Tour de France, which has been marred by blame game politics and well-documented crashes. Top-billed sprinter Caleb Ewan got a few days in before being forced to abandon and injured title contenders Primož Roglič and Geraint Thomas are fighting to get through the pain of simply sitting on their bikes.

This week I've constantly been asked to report on or speak about crashes and specifically the one caused by a spectator during the Grand Départ. A radio producer said to me that crash was the biggest story to come out of the Tour so far, which I admonished until I saw that even American rapper 50 Cent had weighed in on it over Twitter.

When a journalist in the press room said race organiser ASO had flagged up suing the woman I thought it was too preposterous to be true. Yet the organization, until withdrawing its complaint a day after she was taken into police custody, did contribute to a witch hunt that wasn't as interested in the devastating pile-ups that followed, none of which, FYI, were caused by fans.

No one is threatening to sue the teams or riders who have come down this week through a touch of wheels, or taking too many risks. No one has ventured to say ASO, or the UCI should be publicly vilified and prodded with metaphorical pitchforks for creating and condoning a *parcours* that riders – too little and too late – have raised safety concerns over. The course came out on November 1 and, even if you can't change it the peloton can manage how it is tackled. Why didn't riders on stage three, having stated at the start that the approach to the finish was dangerous, neutralise proceedings on the areas they deemed too much? Ewan, Thomas and Roglič all came down in separate incidents that day.

"It was quite a big crash. It's easy to talk myself into it, 'I'm OK blah, blah, blah.' But it still takes a lot out of you, as you can see with Roglič as well. I'm suffering," Thomas said after stage seven. The Welshman and Roglič have not hidden how much pain they are in, and it was evident on stage eight, the first foray into the mountains, when they fell back to the last group on the road.

Roglič's Jumbo-Visma team has been focused on recovery for days now. "[Defending Tour champion Tadej] Pogačar was already the favourite but for now it's enormous, his position. I would say there is only one top favourite left," admitted Jumbo-Visma sports director Merijn Zeeman.

"Teams will make their tactics and see if they can come back to him. But also, regarding the last TT in Saint-Émilion, it's clear everyone needs at least one minute on him before we are there, and I think that's how it looks now and for us. For now, we only recover, and we don't want to think too much about what will come or what we can do. We just need to recover from all the crashes now."

The go-slow protest at the beginning of stage four dominated pre-race interviews but it was meek at best. Not all teams agreed with it and even figureheads of the sport, like Peter Sagan, were resigned. "What is going to change?" said Sagan. "The riders we have to change our mind otherwise it's going to get only worse. Nothing is going to change anyway. The last 10 years it's only worse and worse."

Fans cause crashes, sometimes with no intent, as was the case with the woman with the cardboard sign, and sometimes through incredibly bad, dare I say idiotic, judgement. But the fact is that the industry is quick to judge them, to point fingers and avoid accountability when it is at fault for dangerous spills and cheap thrills. That's an embarrassment.

This week I should have been reporting on Mathieu van der Poel's family lineage that made his tenure in the yellow jersey so special. I should have been talking about the workings behind Mark Cavendish's comeback from the bin, or young Pogačar's command. The politics and lack of unity between industry parties, even between riders, is as much to blame for the broken bones, horrifying carnage, skinned backsides and concussions suffered this week.

"Nothing will change unless they change the rules. It's as simple as that," said BikeExchange sports director Matt White. "This is the biggest event of the year and people are all just looking out for themselves. "Talking to our guys in the bus as well, there is a general lack of respect for each other in the peloton. There are guys who are taking a lot of risks. You hear stories from the guys of people pushing each other out of the way, grabbing each other. That didn't fly that long ago."

The way the Tour is romanticized doesn't help. Slandering people who cause crashes and then celebrating the portrayal of riders as hard nut gladiators with a tough, ride or die attitude seems counterintuitive. They're people. And broken bones can quickly turn into broken minds, which even riders sometimes seem to forget.

In a press release following *that* stage one crash in which Marc Soler suffered multiple arm fractures, Movistar opened its communication around the incident saying, "the Tour de France honoured its macabre legend in the opening week". That's open to translation and interpretation but romanticizing a crash in which one of your riders was badly injured, and then more so putting said mangled rider back on his bike achieves what exactly? Macabre, yes. Legendary? No.

Soler finished the stage despite not being able to take his own jersey off afterwards. "The fall happened at a point in the race where the road narrowed, and we were trying to be well-placed… The mechanic pulled me up by my armpits, and I sat on the side of the road, I was really dizzy. There were still 50 kilometres to go," he told *La Vanguardia*. "[Movistar] told me to try to go on but I don't know how I did, I couldn't change gear or brake. When I got to the finish, I was worried about the time limit, but I couldn't even get my clothes off in the bus, they had to cut them off with scissors."

Why didn't Soler stop? Why did his team even entertain the idea of putting him back on his bike? Where were the UCI medical protocols that should have forbidden it?

Blood doesn't need to be spilt for the Tour to be entertaining or gripping. Fans need to be educated about the dangers of standing too close to the peloton and the importance of giving it space, especially at an event as significant and crucial to the careers of riders and the finances that underpin of the sport. But cycling needs to stop celebrating brutality over common sense. Fans cause crashes, but so do riders, so too do stakeholders through course design, and so too does the UCI for the rules that affect how the Tour is raced. Cycling needs to get a grip.

MAJESTIC MOLLEMA AND THE MOYENNE MONTAGNE

By Nick Bull, July 11 2021

There's a noticeable conflict within Bauke Mollema. What the Dutchman lacks in style when he's riding aggressively on a bike, he makes up for in the substance of those truly spectacular performances he has produced seemingly once or twice a year throughout his career. As he soloed to win Saturday's Tour de France stage in Quillan from a long-range attack, Mollema's open-mouthed, tongue out, square-hipped dancer style only disappeared as he started celebrating 1,300 metres from the line.

This was as much a dominant victory – he finished 1min 4sec ahead of runner-up Patrick Konrad (Bora-hansgrohe) and 12 other breakaway riders – as it was a necessary one: Trek-Segafredo's last triumph in the Tour came three years ago. "Oh, it's super nice," said Mollema. "It's amazing to win a stage again. It was a nice group, [with] a lot of strong guys, [but] a few guys were not really turning. I was feeling good so I just thought 'let's go from far'. I was feeling good and I had the confidence that I could ride alone and keep going for a long time. Normally I can pace myself pretty well. It was a hard final but I'm super happy I made it."

Today's *parcours* looked perfectly suited to a breakaway, and yet it took 85 lively kilometres before the race-winning move – instigated by Wout Poels (Team Bahrain Victorious) and Mattia Cattaneo (Deceuninck-Quick Step) on the lower slopes of the category two Col de Montségur – began to take shape. Even then, it took Mollema's chase group another 13 kilometres to bridge across.

The placement of the Col de Saint-Louis (4.7 kilometres long, 7.4% average gradient), the top of which came 16.9 kilometres from the finish, was the obvious launchpad for attacks. Instead, Mollema reached its summit with a minute gap, having accelerated on the descent of the Côte de Galinagues a little over 40 kilometres out. "He's a great rider – he used his experience today," said Sergio Higuita (EF Education Nippo), who finished third. "We've seen that before in many races. When I saw it was him who was attacking I knew it was a danger."

Admittedly, things were more sedate in the peloton, even with the presence of Cofidis rider Guillaume Martin in the front group. The Frenchman has jumped to second overall and now lies 4min 4sec behind race leader Tadej Pogačar. "I enjoyed every moment of it," said the *maillot jaune,* as he moved another day nearer to Paris. Nonetheless, this stage continued the recent trend of medium mountain stages at the Tour being must-watch television.

Who can forget Thomas De Gendt's solo victory and the brilliant Julian Alaphilippe attack, which resulted in him reclaiming the yellow jersey after a two-up time trial into the finish with Thibaut Pinot, that illuminated stage eight of the 2019 race into Saint Etienne? That day's 200-kilometre route featured seven categorised climbs, none of which ranked higher than second category.

There was stage two in and around Nice last year, which included one full and one partial ascent of Col d'Eze in the final 45 kilometres. Cue another Alaphilippe headline performance there, too. While a lot of the pre-race talk regarding the seventh stage of the 2021 Tour between Vierzon and Le Creusot centred around its length, *L'Équipe*'s frontpage headline *Un Air De Classique* that morning proved accurate. As it stands, it is the best stage of this edition, in part due to the inclusion of the Signal d'Uchon climb in the closing kilometres.

The Tour's race director Christian Prudhomme has previously spoken highly of *moyenne montagne* stages. At the launch of the

2019 Tour he said: "Our desire is not to make things harder but to vary things. Medium mountains [are] where the race will be harder to control." Asked what his highlights of last year's race were, Prudhomme described the stages into Lavaur, Lyon and Champagnole, all of which featured intermediate terrain, as "great". But cycling's funding model, in which local authorities pay to host stages, will always impact where races go. There's a reason why any article detailing somebody's dream Tour de France route will only ever amount to a fantasy. The history and appeal of the legendary mountains will also be hard to resist.

What happened in Saturday's stage and, more so, during the enthralling day of racing to Le Creusot last Friday, is not proof that medium mountain stages are guaranteed thrillers. Both were helped somewhat by their positioning in the race – immediately before the first true Alpine and Pyrenean stages – and following some particularly gruelling days of racing. Were more of this type of stage to be included at the expense of true mountain stages, it's possible that the unpopular suffocating tactics, often undertaken by the team of the yellow jersey wearer, would simply be deployed more aggressively in them. Pogačar's UAE-Team Emirates train may have broken down upon leaving the station on stage seven; today's performance reiterated that they've learned from their mistakes that day.

Nonetheless, stage 14 had plenty going for it. Mollema's early attack may have lessened the importance of the day's final climb, the Col de Saint-Louis, but it allowed the *France Télévisions* director to show it off in all its glory to a worldwide audience. Reminiscent of Sa Calobra in Mallorca, its quirky viaduct bend and challenging-but-not-severe characteristics surely mean that the Tour will return to climb it for only the second time in race history before too long. The stage also reignited the King of the Mountains competition, which is now being led by Michael Woods (Israel Start-Up Nation). The Canadian's chances of topping the standings into Monday's second rest day may depend on how much his crash on the Galinagues descent shortly before Mollema attacked takes out of him tomorrow. Naturally, Mollema's win means that Trek-Segafredo can rest a little easier now. A race that had heralded nine top-10 finishes in 13 stages was transformed into something resembling a success in the space of four hours and 16 minutes. But arguably the biggest winner was the intermediate terrain: how many of the race's next four stages in the high mountains will be as good as this one?

BENIGN VENTOUX ON A DAY TO REMEMBER

By Peter Cossins, July 7 2021

I live in the mountain because I love the mountains. Any mountains. The sight of any massif rising up from the plains triggers a desire to climb, by bike or on foot. Some mountains, though, have a particular attraction and Mont Ventoux is one of them. In *Mountains of the Mind*, Robert Macfarlane, a climber of the Hillary/Messner/Bonnington variety rather than the Bahamontes/Van Impe/Quintana, describes the Provençal peak as "benign", highlighting it only for the fact that it is the location of the first recorded mountain climb, by the Italian scholar and poet Petrarch, who climbed it in the company of his brother and two servants on 26 April 1336.

For a climber of the highest peaks, like Macfarlane, that description is undoubtedly fitting, but in my own experience the Ventoux is often far from benign. I vividly remember the cloudless day that I drove my family to the summit feeling the wind pick up in intensity as we ascended its barren slopes above Chalet Reynard. Approaching the summit, we saw cyclists walking down because the gusts were so frighteningly strong. Turning the final hairpin towards the summit, a rider was blown backwards almost onto the bonnet of our car. At the top, the conditions were so wild that my wife and young daughter stayed in the car because they were worried about being picked up by the wind and swept away into the void.

Cycling, of course, has a well-recorded history of battles on the Ventoux and with the elements, of deathly heat in 1955 and 1967, of the terrifying wind in 2016 that forced the organisers to move the finish 7km down the mountain to Chalet Reynard. There's no other climb in the cycling world where the weather reports are checked with such regular frequency in the days and hours leading up to a race. Yet, today the Tour was blessed with conditions that were about as benign as they get.

Like almost every one of the previous 10 stages in this extraordinary Tour de France, there was so much to take in, talking points aplenty. It would be totally amiss not to start with the winning performance of Wout van Aert, who in his post-stage press conference described his victory as "probably the best of my career, because of the way I did it, by finishing alone on a mountain stage at the Tour de France, which is definitely not something I expected a few years ago, and because it's an iconic mountain in the Tour, a place with a lot of history."

Part of the 17-rider breakaway that clipped away early on in the stage, the Belgian champion was happy to let others set the tempo initially and then held back when Trek-Segafredo's Kenny Elissonde made the initial jump from the breakaway on one of the Ventoux's steepest ramps in the forest beneath Chalet Reynard. When van Aert made his move a few hundred metres later, he looked so strong and smooth that Elissonde's plucky bid for glory instantly looked doomed. The Frenchman hung on for three kilometres, then gradually ceded.

Once clear on his own, van Aert's was a performance of graceful power, his rhythm constant, his gaze set, looking every inch the champion in his Belgian national jersey. Will it prove to be a turning point in his career, the moment when he realised that a future bid for the yellow jersey might be within his reach?

Behind him, the battle for this year's yellow jersey took a very unexpected turn when van Aert's teammate Jonas Vingegaard attacked and dropped the hitherto impregnable Tadej Pogačar. As the young Dane accelerated away, it struck me to what extent the weather gods were collaborating with the action. Usually on the rise through the Ventoux's lunar landscape above Chalet Reynard, there's a block headwind blowing down from the summit that convinces the riders that there's no point in attacking. Today, however, the wind favoured the brave, coming across or from slightly behind, and Vingegaard made full use of it.

Although the 40-second lead that he built up as he passed beneath the distinctive communications and weather towers at the Ventoux's summit evaporated on the descent, where Pogačar benefited substantially from the support he got from Rigoberto Uran and Richard Carapaz, it offered a glimmer of hope for the GC battle. Will Pogačar's astonishing rides in the opening half of the race undermine his progress in the second half, which features three extremely tough climbs in the Pyrenees? With van Aert and Sepp Kuss as his lieutenants, Vingegaard may yet cause the defending champion a few jitters.

A tip of the hat too for the Trek trio Elissonde, Bauke Mollema and Julian Bernard, who almost carved out a brilliant victory. The latter's presence in the break offered the possibility that the Frenchman might produce a fairytale performance, 34 years after his father Jean-François clinched a famous time trial victory atop the Ventoux. It wasn't to be, but the trio perhaps deserved rather more than Elissonde's prize as the day's most aggressive rider.

As for Ineos, if their goal in setting the pace in the peloton almost all day was to shake out some of Carapaz's rivals for a podium place, the tactic was a success, as David Gaudu and, more notably, Ben O'Connor both lost ground. But it cost them their road captain, Luke Rowe, who finished outside the time limit.

Finally, it's clear that ASO's decision to feature two ascents of the Ventoux for the first time was a huge success. The mountain always adds to the sense of expectation when it appears on the Tour route and this unprecedented stage didn't disappoint. It was, as van Aert said in his press conference, "a very special day".

INEOS FLOUNDER AS WIN PROVES ELUSIVE

By Jeremy Whittle, July 14 2021

Not since the 2014 Tour de France has a Tour de France team run by Sir Dave Brailsford seemed so unsure of itself. So why have Ineos Grenadiers seemed so underpowered, after sweeping almost all before them in the week-long stage races prior to this year's Tour? Less than a year ago, in September 2020, racing in the shadow of the pandemic, there was a glum air hanging over Brailsford's team, personified by defending champion Egan Bernal's pained expression when he finally accepted that his back problems would prevent him from mounting a successful defence of the yellow jersey he had won in 2019.

But you have to go back to 2014, the year of Chris Froome's abandon on the fifth stage to Arenberg, to recall a Sky or Ineos Grenadiers squad that felt so directionless, even meandering, as the Tour entered its final stages. This from a team designed to dominate, a team that wins serial Grand Tours – it doesn't scrap for the podium. "It's no fun when you're not winning," Brailsford told me in Paris in July 2014. It's safe to assume that nothing in his attitude has changed in the intervening years.

Of course the British team still has high hopes of a top three finish for Richard Carapaz, the Ecuadorian that the team are calling "Billy," but who now, with one mountain stage to go, has little hope of toppling the untouchable Tadej Pogačar from his perch at the pinnacle of the world's biggest and baddest bike race. There is no doubt that it has been an odd Tour for Ineos, in which they have blown hot and cold. The tone was set even before the race began when the 'four leader strategy,' was set up in the pre-race press conference with Geraint Thomas, Carapaz, Richie

Porte and Tao Geoghegan Hart, all meeting the media, one by one. Almost immediately a lack of clarity and unity was evident. Tour debutant Geoghegan Hart in particular was irked by one journalist's question, which related the order of appearance in the zoom call, with Thomas coming first, to the team's hierarchy. "I think that's a ridiculous question," Geoghegan Hart said. "Is the first one the best or is the last one the best? But when you leave the room who are you going to be thinking about? The last person you just spoke to." By stage three, the four-pronged tactic was already out of the window, after Geoghegan Hart crashed on stage one and Thomas crashed and dislocated his shoulder on stage three. By that point, Porte was slipping away also and by the time the peloton tackled the first Alpine stage, the reality was that only Carapaz remained in contention.

Mystery has surrounded the team's relations with the media. Brailsford, understandably wary given the recent findings of the Richard Freeman hearing, has avoided all but the most cursory contacts with the press. And then of course, there's 'The Plan.' Did the riders every really buy into the much-vaunted four leader strategy?

"With the team that we have, Pogačar cannot follow all of us," Porte had said in Brest. "There should be four of us up there, hopefully, when we hit the mountains. We have such a strong team. That's our trump card." By the second rest day, Geoghegan Hart was openly dissing the tactic. "You can't protect four riders in the Tour – it's never going to happen," the Londoner said. For a rider who focussed so much on the Tour, maybe his prickly demeanour is understandable. Deprived of the chance to start the Giro d'Italia with the number '1' pinned to his jersey, his Tour debut has been pretty miserable, particularly after his crash on the opening stage.

The loss of Luke Rowe on the Mont Ventoux stage, after the veteran road captain finished outside the time limit, seemed to undermine the old Band of Brothers image, definitively. At times, it did not seem that the team was pulling together. Carapaz, meanwhile, has continued to plough a gutsy but lonely furrow and deserves the podium finish that now seems likely.

Yet if it hadn't been for the Ecuadorian how would this Tour have panned out for Ineos? Without Egan Bernal, with Thomas in his twilight years, and lacking the talismanic qualities that both the late Nico Portal and former team leader Froome gave them, the British team has been strangely anonymous.

The team's two sports directors, Gabriel Rasch and Servais Knaven, have experience and expertise of course, but there is no doubt that the team misses the charismatic Portal hugely. Maybe they even miss Froome, too, whose icy calm and driven nature ensured that his team mates always seemed to be primed, briefed, and on their toes.

Without any stage wins it has been a strange Tour de France for Ineos. It seems now almost certain that this will be the second consecutive Tour in which overall victory has eluded them. This is a team in transition, a team that once dominated, now trying to find its footing again. Brailsford, so disconsolate when Team Sky, sans Froome, failed to succeed in 2014, will be well aware that claiming a podium step is nice, but it's not enough for a franchise that always expects to win.

INSIDE THE TOUR ON A *MOTO*

By Sophie Smith, July 17 2021

Hours after covering stage 19, which Matej Mohorič won, my ears are still ringing. It's difficult to focus. I understand now more than ever what riders mean when they say the sound of silence when they get home from the Tour is part of the recovery process. For about five hours on Friday, it was like my finger was back on the pulse of the Tour and all the challenges of the third week melted away at up to 120km/h.

I'd met my driver, Gaetan Prime, by his motorcycle just up from the start line of stage 19. It was good fortune that Mr Prime was assigned to me because, as his surname may suggest and I know from prior experience, he is an excellent bike handler and I for sure had the best seat in the house on this day. He is also very kind and speaks to me in English as much as possible, forgiving the fact that even in my ninth Tour, I'm ashamed to say, my French is still mediocre at best.

We ride out of Mourenx ahead of the peloton, taking in the sunflower fields that border the roads as the race gets underway. From the start of the 207km transition stage to the end, fans are at the roadside, cheering and waving at everyone involved in the race as they go past. From the home-made signage and chalked roads, you'd think Cyril Gautier and Julian Alaphilippe were local gods. Along the course there's also a few supporters with cardboard posters that are replicas of the one brandished by the spectator who caused *that* crash at the Grand Départ.

But the men, women and children of all ages, who have taken a part of, if not their entire day, to see the Tour roll past, aren't there for a single rider or team. The way they clap, wave and, when the riders fly by, roar, is more in appreciation of the history and nature of the race, the sacrifice it demands, than any one individual.

A breakaway has formed and there is a few minutes between it and the peloton. So Mr Prime begins to duck and dive between the two, following the pace of the race, and navigating the immense traffic around him – riders, other motorbikes, an onslaught of team cars, medical vehicles, commissaires.

The fields give way to the woods and planted pine trees as they race moves on. There are six blue helicopters that fly overheard broadcasting the Tour. They fly high and then low, peeling off, coming back, indicating where the breakaway and the peloton, which is suddenly right beside me, is. The peloton is riding single file and moving in formation like birds on a migration route, right, then left until we are against the barriers but not in danger. The riders don't acknowledge us, but seem to sense we are there.

Something catches my eye as we approach the 'collection zone'. Empty gel wrappers discarded at the drop off point catch in the wind and tumble across the road; they are not of interest to spectators who receive *bidons* as if they're nuggets of gold. Then there is a crash. Mr Prime says he doesn't like the 'collection zone' and it doesn't take a wizard to figure out why.

The hold-up clears as Luke Durbridge waits in the middle of the road for a mechanic, who is fixing his bike. Mark Cavendish and some of his Deceuninck-Quick-Step teammates, Sonny Colbrelli and a select group of others use the convoy to chase back on to the main group. Still amid the pine trees, I am so close to Dan Martin that our shoulders are virtually about to rub. I consider saying hello but then don't. We're travelling on the edge of the road, where dirt meets tarmac and there is a fine dust floating over the peloton.

A bit later, the world champion Alaphilippe drifts back to his second team car on the road and I wonder why he didn't go to the first. He comes back laden with *bidons* as others follow suit. Not even the rainbow jersey is above manual labour in this race.

We transition from open roads through fields and forest onto single, twisting lanes that lead into stone villages rammed with people. Mr Prime knows the rhythm, the language of the race and as the horns of team cars trying to push forward into impossible gaps sound, as the sirens of gendarmes warn, as the sound of race radio instructs sports directors on who needs what and where, he moves as focused, effortlessly and fearlessly as the riders do.

I take a second to appreciate the skill of Mr Prime, the sports directors and everyone else who drives in the convoy. Normal road rules don't apply. It's an ongoing stop, start, accelerate, shout, repeat ensemble. It takes immense concentration: to stay present, stay alert and not focus on how your butt hurts from being in the same spot for five plus hours, or what you want for dinner, or why you were in a shit mood earlier.

The forest gives way to vineyards as we approach the finish behind the breakaway. I stand up on the bike to see the lead group move and counter move before we pull off with 150m to go. I give Mr Prime a hug as he drops me at the mixed zone, where journalists interview riders past the finish line. I will never be able to tell the infinite number of stories of every person from every stage of the Tour but being in a position to see it is magic. Once your ears stop ringing.

THE GOOD, THE BAD AND THE UGLY OF THE 2021 TOUR

By William Fotheringham, July 18 2021

The good, in order of goodness:

Tadej Pogačar. A far more assured three weeks for his second Tour than for his first, backed by a team which, while not comparable to the armadas that supported Chris Froome at Team Sky, was still able to do what was needed when it was needed. The second Tour is the point at which a racer moves from possible fluke to assured champion; many take one Tour, few add a second. The only speck of dust in the Pog-UAE 2021 vintage was stage seven to Le Creusot; they needed a rider in the day's big split, and without one were forced to waste valuable energy keeping the move within reach. And the most impressive thing about Pogačar's No2: it came after winning Liège-Bastogne-Liège and Tirreno-Adriatico.

Mark Cavendish. Not even the glitch which happened on the Champs Elysées can detract from Cav's fabulous Tour. For a rider who didn't know he was riding 10 days before the Tour started, four stage wins was an outstanding outcome, so too the joint stage win record with Eddy Merckx. Cav can stop now, his career complete. But he probably won't, and why should he?
2022: when there will be a first stage of a Women's Tour de France on the Champs Elysées, followed by a week's racing. You can't see how this won't be a game changer. And honestly, the world of cycling has waited long enough for ASO to make a definitive move on this.
Mathieu van der Poel. His stage win at Mûr de Bretagne was a classic piece of racing from the VDP copy book, so too his lead-out the following afternoon at Pontivy to secure Alpecin-Fenix

a second stage win in two days with Tim Merlier. The bravura with which he took the final double bend was quite something.
Insane attacks. Van der Poel on day two; van Aert smashing the move clear en route to Le Creusot; a whole load of bright sparks at kilometre zero in the cross-wind on the road to Nîmes; Alaphilippe at the start of the Ventoux stage; Nils Politt and company on the Libourne stage. And various others, all of whom made for a Tour which was truly compelling at times.
David Gaudu. From vomiting on the Ventoux to pressing hard in the Pyrenées. How could anyone not be impressed? And an honourable mention to all those who stuck their necks out and didn't get any reward.
The bad: *Teams that didn't meet up to expectations:* BikeExchange, Ineos, Astana, DSM, Israel-Start Up Nation.
The Omi and Opi placard. It was an appalling moment. All the worse because there is very little any organiser or rider can do to prevent this kind of idiocy. At times like this, I wondered if I didn't prefer the Tour in a sort of 2020-style semi *huis clos*.
Initiating legal action against the Omi and Opi placard holder, then dropping it. Can't we just be consistent?
The Tokyo Olympics: Too close to the Tour, leading to (notably) Mathieu van der Poel disappearing after a week. You can see why he would do that, but it's reasonable to argue it isn't healthy for the Tour.
La Course by le Tour de France: a great finale, and a great winner in Demi Vollering. But the insanely early start time underlined that this is a race which has always teetered on the edge of being a tokenistic afterthought and occasionally gone over it (I remember one edition where there were rightful complaints about a lack of actual changing rooms or toilets). It won't be much missed.
The ugly: crashes. Simply too many. You can argue all you like that there are or aren't more than there used to be; I thought

there were no more than usual on the first weekend but began to have second thoughts when they were still toppling like flies in week two. But the fact is the guys were still falling off 48 hours from Paris having flipped over like a stack of dominoes time and again in Brittany, not to mention the massively destructive crash en route to Carcassonne.

Crashes deprived the 2021 Tour of: Tony Martin, Peter Sagan, Primož Roglič, Caleb Ewan, Simon Yates and many others. You can't argue the pile-ups didn't materially affect the race. Horror is reasonable, answers, not so simple.

Ineos. Their bizarre tactics indicated they had less than zero notion how to deal with the Pog phenomenon. Plan A: put five riders on the front and get them driving. Plan B: see Plan A. At times, it looked straight out of the 90s "punishment for not being in the break" playbook. Zero risk, minimum reward.

And finally, to end on a Good, Bad, Ugly theme… the coffin full of dollars that Clint and company dig up in the cemetery in Sergio Léone's classic western:

Wout van Aert, and the rest of Jumbo-Visma's "fab four": Sep Kuss, Jonas Vingegaard, Mike Teunissen. To respond as Jumbo-Visma did having lost their leader Primož Roglič and half their team was outstanding, an object lesson in balancing risk and reward. Sending van Aert up the road en route to the Ventoux and Kuss and van Aert up the road en route to Andorra was risky on paper, but amply rewarded. Van Aert's weekend double outlined his status as cycling's consummate all-rounder – a Sean Kelly for the 21st century with cyclo-cross as his added strong suit – but in the Champs Elysées win the work of his lead-out man Mike Teunissen more than merits a mention. Four stage wins and second overall after being deprived of your leader on day two is quite the result for any team.

Chapter Six: Waiting for the Tour de France Femmes

WOMEN'S STAGE RACING TIMELINE

March 30: plans for a six-day Battle of the North stage race in August 2022 are revealed, with six stages across Scandinavia

May 12: Christian Prudhomme confirms there will be a Women's Tour de France in 2022, but prompts criticism for adding, "it mustn't lose money."

May 23: Incredibly, the season is three months old before the first Women's WorldTour stage race. Anna van der Breggen is the winner of the Tour of Burgos, with Annemiek van Vleuten at just 3sec

June 6: Lizzie Deignan takes the inaugural Tour de Suisse Women

July 20: Zwift announces that it will be the title sponsor of the *Tour de France Femmes avec Zwift*, that will be run from July 24-31 in 2022, with the opening stage on the Champs Elysées in conjunction with the finish of the men's Tour de France

August 15: van Vleuten triumphs in the Ladies' Tour of Norway, clinching the win at the summit finish at Norefjell; she is run close by Ashleigh Moolman Pasio, just 39sec behind overall

August 29: Chantal van den Broek-Blaak wins the Simac Ladies Tour (previously the Boels Ladies Tour). Marianne Vos takes two of the five stages, plus the prologue

September 5: van Vleuten lands two mountain stages and the overall in the Ceratizit Challenge by la Vuelta

October 10: Demi Vollering of SDWorx wins the AJ Bell Women's Tour after a dominant time trial victory on stage three. The other stage victories go to Marta Bastianelli, Amy Pieters, Lorena Wiebes and Elisa Balsamo.

NEXT GENERATION DELIGHTS AT GIRO DONNE

By Amy Jones, July 8 2021

The Giro d'Italia Donne has been dominated so far by Anna van der Breggen, who currently leads the race by 2min 51sec from her nearest rival – teammate Ashleigh Moolman Pasio. The world champion is in the form of her life, but she is still adamant that she will retire after this season and pick up her new role as DS for her team, SD Worx.

The question of who will replace van der Breggen and her generation has partly been answered already this season but from watching the Giro Donne, the future is looking bright with talented young riders coming to the fore on all types of *parcours*. The increasing professionalisation of the women's peloton is contributing to the rise of more young talent as riders are able to make cycling their full-time career. So, who are the up and coming talents who are set to take over?

Demi Vollering

The hole that the imperious van der Breggen will leave in her team already looks set to be filled more than comfortably by Demi Vollering. The 24-year-old has shown herself to be more than capable of delivering, which has instilled enough confidence in van der Breggen for the World Champion to ride for her young teammate at the likes of Liège-Bastogne-Liège and La Course – both of which Vollering won.

An all-rounder of similar capability to van der Breggen – but with an even faster finish – Vollering is a real threat to anyone who might have their eye on either a punchy classic or a stage race GC. The question of whether the 24-year-old might be left vulnerable at the pointy end of races in the absence of her experienced compatriot is answered by one glance at an SD Worx squad full of decorated champions waiting to take up the superdomestique mantle.

Niamh Fisher-Black

One such rider waiting in the SD Worx wings is 20-year-old Kiwi Niamh Fisher-Black. The tiny climber possesses an altogether different skillset to her Dutch teammate but is a talented rider in her own right who is currently wearing the white young rider's jersey in the Giro Donne.

Fisher-Black came to prominence last season as the New Zealand national champion. She only managed 22 race days in 2020 but nine of those were at the Giro Rosa, during which she made an impression by riding for teammate Mikayla Harvey to defend her white jersey and taking second on the final stage. Her Giro performance was enough to catch the eye of Danny Stam at SD Worx and Fisher-Black signed a two year contract with the team. The move has proven to be mutually beneficial with the young Kiwi learning from her experienced teammates whilst also frequently making herself useful on the front or in breakaways. There is no doubt that a top result awaits Fisher Black in the future should she be given the opportunity to ride for herself.

Evita Muzic

A similar rider to Fisher-Black, it was Muzic who narrowly edged her out to win that final stage in 2020. To complete the Giro as a 21-year-old with the likes of Annemiek van Vleuten and van der Breggen in the race is an impressive feat in itself, but to retain enough form to win the final stage goes one step further.

This year, Muzic and her FDJ team had a tumultuous start to the race, with leader Cecilie Uttrup Ludwig crashing during the team time trial and the team finishing 1min 46sec down. Muzic has been slowly clawing back time and now sits third in the young rider classification and 14th overall.

The 22-year-old has spent her entire career with FDJ, first joining the team in 2018 at the age of 18. This season, the young French rider will wear her national champion's colours after denying the experienced Trek-Segafredo rider Audrey Cordon Ragot a second year in the jersey at the title race last month.

Mikayla Harvey

Harvey took the young rider's jersey at the 2020 edition of the Giro by 4min 55sec. This year, in the absence of Canyon//SRAM team leader Kasia Niewiadoma, she looked set to lead her team into another strong performance. However, after a solid TTT from her team, the 22-year-old Kiwi lost almost nine minutes on her rivals on the stage two summit finish and lost her GC hopes.

While the GC race she wanted may not have transpired, Harvey can take comfort in an impressive 2021 season belied by her results on paper. The former junior national champion has spent some key races attacking and riding on the front for her team leaders, as well as managing top-10s for herself at the one-day Spanish races in May and last month's Tour de Suisse Women. With another season left on her contract with Canyon//SRAM, Harvey looks set to develop into the type of all-rounder/climber that her team's leader, Kasia Niewiadoma, became before her.

Marta Cavalli

FDJ Nouvelle Aquitaine Futuroscope have a wealth of young talent in their midst, and Italian rider Marta Cavalli is a standout example. An exciting all-rounder, Cavalli has had some impressive results since moving over to the French squad from Valcar Travel and Service.

This season, the 23-year-old has had a series of top-10 results in some big races including 8th at Strade Bianche – after a gutsy attack at the bottom of the final climb – as well as 6th at Flanders.

Her Giro Donne ride this season has been equally plucky when, after losing even more time than the rest of her teammates in the TTT, she moved up 72 places on GC after the summit finish on stage two – coming across the line in fourth place. Had she and her team not experienced such bad luck in the opening team time trial, Cavalli would undoubtedly be sitting comfortably within the top-10 on GC.

Juliette Labous

Juliette Labous will be the sole representative of her country in the women's road race and time trial events at the Tokyo Olympic Games, with French selectors overlooking the more experienced Audrey Cordon Ragot in favour of the DSM rider. Labous is shaping up to be a talented all-rounder with a strong time trial – she won the U23 national title in 2020 – and currently sits 8th overall in the Giro Donne GC thanks to three top-10 finishes including a strong 6th place on the individual mountain time trial. With another summit finish coming up on stage 9, Labous could cement her top-10 results even further if she continues to show the same climbing form.

Lorena Wiebes

It's not just the new generation of climbers and all-rounders who are making their mark at this race. When it comes to fast-finishes Labous's teammate Lorena Wiebes is almost unbeaten this season. Barring some crashes and bad luck, the 22-year-old Dutch rider has claimed nine wins so far this season – including her first Giro Donne stage – and could surpass her total of 14 from 2019.

The former Dutch national champion is one of few pure sprinters in the women's peloton and is well-supported by her

DSM teammates including a talented and decorated sprinter Coryn Rivera. Having already taken the win in the flat run-in to Carugate, Wiebes will have her eye on stage 8 which looks made for her.

Emma Norsgaard

That is, unless Emma Norsgaard can stop her. Wiebes has beaten her Danish colleague three times this season so far but Norsgaard has yet to surpass her Dutch rival's speed. That hasn't stopped her from winning an impressive 10 sprints so far this season, however.

It has been a breakthrough year for the 21-year-old, who moved to Movistar from the now-defunct Equipe Paule Ka. Like Wiebes, she also claimed her first Giro Rosa stage win this week, beating none other than Coryn Rivera and Marianne Vos to cross the line first in Colico. If stage eight comes down to a bunch sprint it is likely to be another head-to-head battle between Wiebes and Norsgaard, and the question will be whether the former Danish national champion can find those extra few watts to finally conquer the DSM rider.

The Dutch dynasty of Anna van der Breggen, Annemiek van Vleuten, and Marianne Vos might not be around forever, but with the young talent coming through in their wake, women's racing looks to be as exciting and dynamic as ever in the years to come.

WILL THE GIRO DONNE EVER CHANGE?

By Amy Jones, July 12 2021

Last year, the Giro Donne was demoted from Women's WorldTour (WWT) status to 2.Pro. Myriad failings led to the UCI taking action, however the deciding factor appeared to be the organiser's failure to provide a live broadcast of the race – a requisite of all WWT races. There were plenty of other issues relating to the general organisation, or lack thereof, and even questions of safety.

Few dared to believe that the race would learn from past mistakes and come back better in 2021, fewer still expected live coverage of the action. The travesty of not being able to watch the toughest race on the women's calendar – the Giro Donne is the longest race at 10 stages – looked set to continue.

Then, in February, a new website emerged boasting of a new and improved version of the race under new organisers PMG Sport. They had an ambitious new plan for a bigger and better version of the Giro, including live coverage, with the overall aim of returning the race to WWT status.

In a statement released on the race website, Giro d'Italia Donne General Director, Roberto Ruini said: "When in February of this year we chose to take on this three-year project, shared with FCI [Italian Cycling Federation], our mission was exactly to bring the Giro back into the Women's WorldTour. After this choice by UCI, we will always continue to give our best, both in terms of organization and production and of media distribution".

It sounded promising, like the race would be turning over a new leaf and waking up to the existential threat posed to it by races such as the upcoming Tour de France Femmes and the Battle of the North. In addition, a race website featuring a road book and details of every stage ahead of time was more than the previous organisers had managed in the past, but the bar was low.

The new organisers also claimed to have 'doubled' the prize money from the previous year, which – while they did increase it – did not turn out to be precisely the case. Unfortunately, €8,000 for the GC winner still pales in comparison to men's races and even some women's races. Of course, that particular topic has already been extensively turned over this season in the wake of Omloop Het Nieuwsblad.

As the race got closer to starting the reality behind the promises was revealed. Yes, there would be live coverage of each stage but it would merely consist of the final 15km and at what time it might start could be anyone's guess. The organisers created a Twitter page but no race updates were provided other than retweets from team accounts.

After the first few stages, it became clear that the duration and timing of the live coverage would be sporadic – ranging from 6km on the first stage to 34km on stage 8. PMG were operating with 4G signals which can be patchy and unreliable in the mountains and the resulting complete lack of live images from the Queen stage to Monte Matajur were reportedly down to signal failure."

On the organisational and safety level, some riders have commented that the race has seen an improvement: "I definitely think that there is a step up, when it comes to the organisation," said Ashleigh Moolman Pasio after winning the Queen stage. However, elsewhere, there were reports of a dangerous neutralised rollout on stage five from Milan, in which the roads were not fully closed and the peloton were forced to ride over large cobblestones through the city centre.

At present, the Giro is on the 2022 WWT calendar, however in a press release, the governing body was adamant that this hinged upon "the 2021 edition meeting the specifications for the series" which includes at least 45 minutes of live coverage among other minimum standards. In its current iteration, the Giro Donne doesn't pass the test.

With the Tour de France Femmes on the way next year, as well as the Battle of the North and the return of The Women's Tour, there are bigger and better options for the women's peloton on the horizon. While confidence in Tour de France organiser ASO's commitment to women's cycling hasn't traditionally been strong, a high-profile race like the Tour de France Femmes must live up to ASO's current standards or risk its reputation. Races that continue to meet, or even surpass, the minimum standards will make the Giro look even more archaic in its laissez faire approach by comparison unless real improvements are actually made by the race. Whether the 2022 edition will keep its WWT slot remains to be seen, but the race's track record doesn't particularly instil confidence in its potential to deliver an event worthy of the increasingly professional women's peloton.

THE KIESENHOFER EFFECT

By Amy Jones, August 2021

As only the second Women's WorldTour level stage race of the season, the Ladies Tour of Norway provided a welcome variation for the peloton and presented opportunities for riders who are usually put to work on behalf of team leaders. Still in a post-Olympic transition period wherein many of the top riders are still enjoying a break after the Games and before the second half of the season, the four-day race threw up some new names on the top step.

To look at the winner of the overall GC – Annemiek van Vleuten – would be to assume that it was business as usual in Norway, but the absence of the likes of Anna van der Breggen, Demi Vollering, and Marianne Vos meant that other riders were given chances they might not usually be presented with.

Kristen Faulkner's move on stage one appeared to be a direct product of The Anna Kiesenhofer Effect. Perhaps inspired by the Austrian Olympic Champion, Faulkner left her breakaway companions behind with 20km to go, staying solo for three laps of the finishing circuit and taking her first ever WorldTour win. The Tibco-SVB rider has been showing great promise since she burst onto the scene at her first UCI race last September – after giving up a career as a Venture Capitalist in Silicon Valley – but a win had eluded her. The 28-year-old American has shown her natural athleticism but had also been known to make some tactical misjudgements in the past, this time, however, she got it just right.

It wasn't just Faulkner who seized her chance to win, however. In the absence of Marianne Vos, Team Jumbo-Visma might have found themselves somewhat directionless at this race. The Dutchwoman has won the Ladies Tour of Norway three times but opted to sit out this year's edition, leaving room for other riders on the team to take chances they might not usually be given space to take whilst working for the leader.

26-year-old Riejanne Markus seized her opportunity on stage two, bridging a one-minute gap to the front group with 47km to go. After the rest of the breakaway started to drop it looked like Markus, who was left in front alone, was doomed with 25km to go, but in another move reminiscent of the new Olympic Champion she carried on her effort and stayed away to the line, upsetting the sprinters and taking her first WWT win.

Norway also saw the return of Chloe Hosking to the peloton after the Australian sprinter was sidelined by Covid in March. With the support of her team, Trek-Segafredo, Hosking returned to the startline last week which would have been seen as a win in itself for many, but the 30-year-old showed that she is not only back in the bunch but back on top by winning the bunch sprint on stage four. Hers is a comeback story of the kind most athletes dream of and Hosking described taking a win in her first race back for four months as "surreal". Hosking will undoubtedly feature prominently in the coming races.

Stage three may have bucked the trend, featuring an 11km climb to the finish which had Annemiek van Vleuten's name written all over it, but although the Dutchwoman took the win and sealed off the GC there were a number of impressive rides behind her. Notably, Swiss rider Marlen Reusser, fresh from taking silver at the Olympic Games in the time trial, and 21-year-old Niamh Fisher Black who looks set to step up with Team SD Worx. The excitement in Norway served to highlight the dearth of stage racing on the Women's WorldTour calendar but also set the stage for an exciting 2022 which will feature – amongst other multi-day events such as the Tour de France Femmes – a revamped version of the same race dubbed The Battle of the North and extended to six stages. As for the rest of this year – with Simac Ladies Tour, Ceratizit Challenge by La Vuelta and the AJ Bell Women's Tour still to come – the second part of the season might be marked as a time for the opportunists to come through.

NEED FOR SPEED

By Amy Jones, August 31 2021

The post-Olympics part of the season is a frustrating time to be a sprinter in the women's pro peloton. With a series of stage races post-Tokyo looking promising for the chances of at least a few sprint showdowns, the return of the battle between the two young rivals, Lorena Wiebes and Emma Norsgaard, looked set. It wasn't to be, however. Because while it's a bad time to be a sprinter, it's a great time to be a chancer. A rider who thrives on the challenge of a high risk, high reward breakaway.

It started with Anna Kiesenhofer at the Olympic Games, then at the Ladies Tour of Norway it was Kristen Faulkner and Riejanne Markus who continued the trend to take their first Women's WorldTour wins. Chloe Hosking took what could have been the last chance for the sprinters for a while on stage four in her first race back since March after a case of Covid. Next, at the Simac Ladies Tour a gutsy breakaway ride by Alison Jackson and Maëlle Grossetête yielded a first win for Jackson, too, thwarting the sprint finish and leaving Wiebes to settle for third.

Stage three of Simac should have ended in a bunch sprint – and was heading in that direction – before a huge crash took down the majority of the peloton. The remaining six women were not so much a breakaway as a group of well-positioned and lucky riders who avoided the carnage. Strewn across the narrow Dutch farm roads was a who's who of the peloton's top-tier sprinters, Lorena Wiebes, Emma Norsgaard, Chloe Hosking, Kirsten Wild, and Alice Barnes.

The unfortunate incident not only left some of the fastest women in the bunch nursing varying degrees of injury and skin loss but also robbed Wild of her last chance at a bunch sprint in her road career. The 38-year-old has 109 career wins to her name on the road, a number that is now set in stone as – even if she were not injured from the crash – her team, Ceratizit-WNT, were forced out of the race with a Covid positive.

The final stage of Simac would have seen a similar showdown to the one we were headed for on stage three had Wiebes, Norsgaard, Wild, and Hosking not already exited the race. As it happened, Marianne Vos gave yet another display of her sheer dominance on all terrains by outsprinting Barnes to take her third win of the tour.

Since July, when at least three stages of the Giro Donne resulted in a bunch kick to the line, the fast finishers of the peloton have had very few subsequent opportunities to battle it out. Women's cycling doesn't lend itself to specialists in the same way as the men's side of the sport. Few riders can truly be labelled as 'pure' anything but Wiebes in particular is the closest to a 'pure sprinter' that the women's peloton has. For her and others like her, there are very few chances remaining for them to unleash their strengths this season.

The cancellation of the Tour of Guangxi and Tour of Chongming Island spelled even further disaster for the chances of pure spritners. The pan-flat races are usually a chance for fast-finishers to sweep a stage race in a way that they usually aren't able to. As it stands, there are just a few days of racing left on the calendar that are likely to come down to a sprint – if a breakaway doesn't get there first. They are: stage four of the Ceratizit Challenge by La Vuelta – although riders need to first navigate two hilly road stages and a mountain time trial – and perhaps a stage or two of The Women's Tour, as well as Ronde van Drenthe at the end of October. The World Championships course is the flattest for a long time but couldn't be considered a pure sprinter's race.

Of course, there are still lower-ranked events to choose from but, when it comes to the Women's WorldTour, it looks like the best chance for success as a sprinter between now and November is to get into a break, and make it stick.

THE BEST FORM OF DEFENSE IS ATTACK

By Amy Jones, September 6 2021

The first edition of the Ceratizit Challenge by La Vuelta came about the year after the inaugural La Course and was a similar type of race – a women's event tacked onto a city centre circuit race on the final day of the men's grand tour. Unlike it's French counterpart, however, the Ceratizit Challenge – or Madrid Challenge as it was formerly known – has grown in length and stature since its inception.

Now four stages long and incorporating a challenging, mountainous *parcours*, this year's edition was one in a series of three stage races in quick succession for the women's peloton, beginning with the Ladies Tour of Norway in early August, followed a week later by Simac Ladies Tour in Holland, before the Ceratizit Challenge began just a few days later.

Annemiek van Vleuten cemented her position as the strongest woman in the peloton by some margin at this race. If the mix up at the Olympic road race galvanized her into her gold medal time trial ride it has positively catapulted her into the latter part of the season.

With her nearest rival, Anna van der Breggen, appearing to enter the latter part of the season – and her career – with a slower build up, van Vleuten took the overall at both Norway and Ceratizit. It's not that the 38-year-old Dutchwoman had nobody challenging her. Rival teams and the best of the peloton were there to take it to her as best they could – it just wasn't enough.

The racing played into the Movistar rider's hands in Spain. A breakaway containing Swiss national champion Marlen Reusser went up the road and gained almost two minutes on the peloton, meaning on the second stage's 7.3km hilly individual time trial van Vleuten had a carrot to chase in the shape of the Swiss. After the stage, van Vleuten claimed not to like stage racing as much as one-day races: "I don't like defending," she said. "I struggle when I have to use that defending attitude in stage races. In my heart, I'm an attacker, I don't like racing conservatively."

Nobody would ever accuse the former world champion of racing conservatively. Van Vleuten is renowned for her sustained solo attacks and constant attempts to snap the elastic and get away from the bunch to use her superior time trial skills. The following day, on stage three, she did exactly that.

"Tomorrow, I have nothing to lose and everything to win," went the European champion's warning shots after the time trial. "I just hope other teams think like that, so we won't give it as a present to Marlen Reusser, make things hard for her to win and offer a good show for people watching on TV tomorrow."

Far from giving Reusser a "present", van Vleuten cast herself as the Grinch Who Stole the GC, escaping from the peloton on a climb after a technical descent and going solo with 40km to go. An elite group containing Elisa Longo-Borghini, Kasia Niewiadoma, Elise Chabbey, Marta Cavalli, Floortje Mackaij, Kata Blanka Vas, Liane Lippert, and Reusser couldn't reel the Women's WorldTour leader back in and she won by a margin of 2min 48sec.

It may not have been the spectacle that van Vleuten hoped to give viewers but she took up the role of attacker with textbook aplomb to claim the general classification lead going into the final stage. She eventually won by the 1:34 margin she ended with on that day after Reusser failed to gain time back on stage four.

It wasn't purely the van Vleuten show at the Ceratizit Challenge. Belgian champion Lotte Kopecky's return to racing after crashing in the Omnium in Tokyo saw her win the final stage and provided a taste of her form going into a home World Championships on a course that suits her.

Elsewhere, SD Worx's young Hungrian talent, Kata Blanka Vas – straight off the back of 5th place in the U23 race at the mountain bike World Championships the week before – put in impressive rides on stages three in her first road race outside of nationals for 2021. Days after her 20th birthday, Vas claimed ninth overall, the best-placed rider on her team.

Third-placed on the general classification, Elise Chabeby of Canyon/SRAM continued her campaign to transition from worker to leader. The Swiss rider's style is not dissimilar to van Vleuten's and Reusser's – all three examples of the fact that riding aggressively pays in women's cycling.

Reusser herself is looking like the biggest threat to van Vleuten for the time trial at the World Championships. After taking silver in Tokyo in that event Reusser has built on her form to put herself on the map as one of the strongest riders in the women's peloton right now. With few races remaining before the fight for the rainbow jersey gets underway, the time trial looks to be van Vleuten's for the taking and, although the course may not suit her, she can never be discounted for the road race either. The question is: who can stop her and will they pull it off?

IN PRAISE OF THE WOMEN'S TOUR

By William Fotheringham, October 5 2021

Seven and a half years pass quickly. It was Wednesday May 7 2014 when I wandered around the back streets of Oundle, all honey coloured limestone and elegant architecture reflecting the small East Midland town's status as one of the few of the UK's Public School towns. I was waiting for the first edition of the Women's Tour to start. There weren't many media there, but there was a relatively large public turnout considering it was a Wednesday morning in Oundle and there were plenty of folk coming out to watch during the 58 mile stage to Northampton won by Emma Johansson. And there was a feeling, I wrote then, that this could be a game changer.

Now backed by AJ Bell, the Women's Tour feels like a fixture in the calendar to the extent that its absence has been sorely felt. It's been two and a half years since it last took place; the 2020 edition fell foul of the Pandemic like most of the UK road racing calendar and the 2021 race has been postponed from its usual early summer slot. Together with the UK national championships on October 17, it pushes the British calendar deep into the autumn, so let's hope the weather gods are smiling. It's worth looking back to May 2014 and reflecting on what has changed and what hasn't. Back in 2014, the notion that a women's race might have the same prize money and working conditions (road closure, accomodation) as the equivalent men's race – in this case the men's Tour of Britain – seemed radical: it was the Women's Tour's USP.

The man behind the race, Guy Elliott, stuck his neck out on this one. The organisers, Sweetspot, also brought it in for their RideLondon Classic. The Women's Tour de Yorkshire followed suit, more impetus came from Flanders Classics, and now it's seen as the standard to which all races should aspire.

In May 2014, as part of the *Guardian's* build-up to the Tour of Britain, Lizzie Armitstead (now Lizzie Deignan) lamented the lack of television coverage of the biggest races such as Flèche Wallonne. "I'm sure we will be on Eurosport one day," said Armitstead. That seems an incredible comment given the expansion in Eurosport's coverage.

It's a measure of how poorly the sport was shown on television that daily coverage for the Women's Tour seemed a big, important step; now the question is not whether, but how much – and the disappointment that greeted the decision not to have live coverage of the race make it clear that the goalposts have moved here too. Again, Flanders Classics and ITV4 have played key roles, with the British broadcaster covering the Tour de Yorkshire and Women's Tour from the get-go.

Back in 2014, there was finally some momentum in the campaign for equality. Armitstead's vocal criticism of cycling's structure after the 2012 London Olympic road race had brought the issue centre stage. The UCI had a new president, Brian Cookson, who had made rapid (if obvious) moves in the domain. *Le Tour Entier* had achieved partial success with the announcement that spring that ASO would inaugurate La Course by Le Tour de France. Back then, this was seen as a stepping stone to a women's Tour de France; it's taken time, but finally that step is to be taken.

Deignan and her team Trek-Segafredo have taken their sport forward, pushing for proper treatment if a racer decides to combine career and family. The inception of the riders' union, The Cyclists' Alliance has played a big role too since its foundation in 2017, raising key questions and pressing for its members interests. Again, none of this was there in May 2014.

There is an element of *plus ça change, plus c'est la même chose*, beyond the fact that Deignan and Marianne Vos are still among the sport's flagship names, which is testament to their drive and class. Back in 2014, there was criticism of Team Sky and British Cycling for failing to invest in, respectively, a women's WorldTour team, and a proper support programme for riders such as Armitstead. There are still WorldTour teams and managers that aren't interested, and still dumb, sexist comments from high-placed men who should know better.

Autumn 2021 feels like another time of rapid progress. On October 14 we will find out where the Women's Tour de France will go after its start on the Champs Elysées next year. It now seems like an aberration for a men's WorldTour team not to have a women's programme run in paralell; Cofidis announced their new team line-up recently, taking the number of French teams to four. The women's transfer market looks healthier than I can remember with new squads like Uno-X vying for riders. Just this year, the Swiss have come on board with the Tour de Suisse and Tour de Romandie.

Back in 2014, I interviewed the then manager of Wiggle-Honda, Rochelle Gilmore, in an attempt to put some perspective on the arrival of La Course and the Women's Tour. "In another 10 years we will be close to parity," was Gilmore's view. The sport isn't close to parity, and there's no room for complacency, but it now seems achievable and the pathway is there. We must never ignore the sport's long history of inequality and sexism but it would be equally blind not to stop occasionally and note the progress that has happened. That low-key race start seven years ago in that honey-stone little town is part of that, and it's good to see the Women's Tour back again.

Alex Broadway/SWpix.com

Alex Broadway/SWpix.com

Alex Whitehead/SWpix.com

Simon Wilkinson/SWpix.com

Alex Whitehead/SWpix.com

Alex Whitehead/SWpix.com

Alex Broadway/SWpix.com

Alex Broadway/SWpix.com

Tim van Wichelen/Cor Vos/SWpix.com

Chapter Seven: Primož and the Power of Three

VUELTA TIMELINE

August 14: Primož Roglič takes the opening time trial in Burgos
August 15: Jesper Philipsen gives Alpecin stage wins in all three Grand Tours in one year when he wins the sprint finish in Burgos
August 17: Fabio Jakobsen completes an incredible comeback with stage victory at Molina de Aragon, 12 months after his horrific crash in Poland
August 24: Michael Storer takes his second stage win of the race for DSM; the leader's jersey is "loaned" by Primož Roglič to Odd Christian Eiking of Intermarché
August 28: Romain Bardet takes his first Grand Tour stage win since 2017 at Pico Villuercas
September 1: After following a long-range attack from Egan Bernal, Roglič wins the stage to Lagos de Covadonga, and deposes Eiking. The Vuelta is effectively over after Bernal loses 95sec
September 3: Magnus Cort Nielsen lands his third stage win of the 2021 race at Monforte de Lemos
September 4: Clément Champoussin gives Ag2R Citroen an unlikely win at Castro de Herville, while Miguel Angel López has a disastrous stage, drops off the podium, and withdraws unexpectedly from the race, prompting his departure from Movistar
September 5: Roglič wins the final time trial into Santiago de Compostela, taking the overall from Enric Mas and Jack Haig

THE SPEAR OR THE TRIDENT?

By Lars B Jørgensen, August 22 2021

History may have taught us that a cycling team is run by spearheaded leadership. The patron. The boss. The complete package. The strong and visionary commander in charge at the Grand Tours. There is a solid logic to all this. The demands in terms of support and balance within a team may dictate that sole leadership is the way to go.

And then – of course – there is the fact that one man can be head and shoulders above the rest of the crop. It's been 35 years since Bernard Hinault and Greg LeMond left a mark on the issue of leadership that has cast very long shadows. The Tour de France 1986 showed that two great riders within a team, with completely different personas, may clash in a way that can be almost counterproductive.

Fuelled by ambition, a desire to win and brilliance galore, LeMond and Hinault created a spectacle that has shaped the way we see any sort of shared leadership within the same team – in their case the mighty La Vie Claire. The young American prodigy and the seasoned French warhorse showed a competitiveness and a rivalry that lit up the race. Exciting, intriguing, dramatic. A gift for all spectators who, for decades to come, could interpret the moves and motives that fired up such contrasting personalities on the road.

It's a fun fact that Paul Köchli, the La Vie Claire team's Swiss coach and DS, actually wanted to build a team that was strong enough in depth to win the Tour no matter who did it. That mission was indeed accomplished. La Vie Claire dominated the Tour de France 1986 with a 1-2 podium top in LeMond and Hinault plus Andy Hampsten and Niki Rüttiman placed 4th and 7th respectively. And yet the fierce and relentless nature with which LeMond and Hinault went to war is still shaping the way we see captaincy in cycling.

The '90's gave us teams like Banesto where Indurain was seated like the embodiment of an Easter Island statue clad in yellow. After 1991, Big Mig's position was never questioned, although it's argued that he should have been leader in the 1990 Tour rather than domestique to Pedro Delgado. He delivered his five Tour victories on the dot. And then there were the seven long years of Lance Armstrong's bullying, where the power was even more monopolized and never contradicted.

Between those two blocks of dominance we may have had some sparkling issues between 1996 Tour winner Bjarne Riis and the German *Jahrhunderttalent* Jan Ullrich at Team Deutsche Telekom. But Riis' powers were already waning the year after his one and only victory and even in 1996 it was clear to see that it was only a matter of time before Ullrich would be the force of nature he showed in 1997.

The question of rivalry and potential treachery is a sort of journalistic Viagra. There are just more tension and emotions at stake when egos clash than when you see a team where the leadership question is sorted, done and dusted.

Movistar is a team that have tried to field a three-headed leadership in recent years, and failed. In 2019 the "Trident" of Nairo Quintana, Mikel Landa and Alejandro Valverde all finished in the top 10 at the Tour without looking like a serious challenge in terms of overall victory. Or even a credible stab at the podium.

The tactics at Movistar are often a matter of head scratching for a lot of the wrong reasons. And as documented in the entertaining Netflix documentary from the seasons 2019 and 2020 the management of the Movistar team seems a bit out of tune if not a shambles. Movistar had another go at this years Tour with Miguel Angel López, Valverde and Enric Mas. The latter showed his gritty consistency while López crashed and even Valverde may be coming to realize that age can be a factor. For Ineos the 2021 Tour may best be remembered as a sort of implosion. The crashes of week one robbed the scarily strong line up of Richard Carapaz, Tao Geoghegan Hart, Richie Porte and Geraint Thomas of both power and tactical agility. What looked like a unit that could cause the stratospheric Slovenian (and now double Tour winner) Tadej Pogačar a few problems never really came into play.

In the Vuelta Ineos are giving it another go with a three-pronged strategy consisting of Carapaz, Bernal and Adam Yates. No leader is designated beforehand. The road will decide. And the legs as well. "That will prevail over what we want personally" as Carapaz put it before the start in Burgos on Saturday. There is a rather childlike logic at stake here. The road and the history books have shown us that it may be a tad more complicated than that when two very strong riders are trying to work out the captaincy between them.

Just think about the tricky Wiggins-Froome situation in 2012. Froome wanted to attack in the Alps and at the Peyresourde finish at the times when Wiggins was struggling a little. There was not much love lost between the two. And personal relationships are always at stake in those kind of situations.

The same could be said about CSC-Saxo Bank in the Tour de France 2008 where Carlos Sastre attacked at l'Alpe d'Huez and never looked back in yellow. The Spaniard rode on a team where Andy and Fränk Schleck were the obvious darlings of general manager Bjarne Riis and DS Kim Andersen. Sastre was destined to put the first attack in before Fränk Schleck went on the counter. But it never happened. And although the team routinely praised Sastre's victory there were some sulky faces at the campfire afterwards. The solid and easy going Sastre left the team at the end of the season after having won Riis and Team CSC their first and only Tour de France.

At a time when some of the top teams like UAE and Bora-Hansgrohe are stacking up talents and GC prospects, they probably will need leadership which is able to connect rather than divide. Ineos showed what might be possible in the 2021 Giro but Covid-19 and a cramped race program also was a factor here. As usual, the road will provide us some answers and fresh perspectives before the Vuelta finishes in Santiago de Compostela on September 5th.

Lars B. Jørgensen is a columnist at Danish national newspaper Berlingske, *the founder of cycling podcast* Souplesse *and sometimes a cyclist* con amore.

AUSSIE CLIMBERS ON LONG ROAD TO THE TOP

By Sophie Smith, August 25, 2021

No Australian has won one of cycling's three Grand Tours since Cadel Evans triumphed at the Tour de France 10 years ago. If you put to one side the success of Richie Porte, only the second Australian to make the Tour podium apart from Evans, you could argue that in the last decade it's been Australia's prolific *puncheurs* and sprinters, more so than climbers, have not exclusively but predominately flown the flag in the WorldTour.

There's a long list of climbers and time trial specialists who have been touted as Evans' successor and certainly been capable of it, but if it has yet to happen. Speaking to me around the 10th anniversary of his Tour win earlier this summer, Evans paused when I asked him why that no Australian had won the *maillot jaune* since his Tour win.

"Um, that's a good question," he said. "I go back to this: at a grassroots level; cycling in Australia isn't very welcoming to climbers and non-sprinters. So, our talent pool of guys who can ride for GC is quite small. Not that we don't have a big talent pool in Australia, but maybe they're taking up running or they're not doing sport at all."

Traditionally, the men's under-23 academy program has been rooted in track cycling. Porte and Ben O'Connor, who celebrated a solo stage victory in Tignes and finished fourth overall at the Tour in July, both progressed through domestic pathways and not the academy that they described individually as a "boy's club".

"[In] Australia, AFL, basketball, you have to be tall. For someone like me, school sport wasn't very encouraging," Evans continued. The sport itself – outside of the Tour – also isn't mainstream in Australia. AFL, rugby league and cricket dominate the headlines. You learn to play those three games, in addition to netball, tennis, basketball and swimming at school or in leagues on weekends. At least where I came from. I rode my bike as a kid every weekend with my family, but it didn't occur to me until I was assigned to report on the 2010 Road World Championships that cycling was a professional sport.

It's a longer road to the top for Australian climbers, but this year you could argue that the tide is changing. Not so much if you look at the newspapers. It's currently footy finals time and almost the cricket season; you'd have to make a compelling case to get column inches for cycling in the mainstream press. But it's Australian climbers rather than sprinters or *puncheurs* that I've been commissioned to speak or write about during and since the Tour.

Jack Haig, long touted in Australian cycling circles as a prodigious talent, lost time on stage nine of the Vuelta a España and dropped from fourth to sixth but is still in the mix for a top 10 result. Michael Storer, in his fifth participation at the Vuelta, celebrated his second stage win of the 2021 edition on Tuesday, perfectly executing a plan from within the breakaway with his DSM team.

I had to get around O'Connor's entire life story quickly at the Tour, where BikeExchange blooded another Australian climber in Lucas Hamilton for GC. They all comprise part of a new generation too far removed from Evans's era to bear the public pressure of following in his footsteps. But they're old enough to remember the competitive feats of the Australian great and perhaps be motivated by that in a more encouraging way.

"Finally, we're coming through with some more of these guys," said Evans. "Hopefully back 10 years ago I inspired someone, who is going to be coming through the ranks now, or five years' time, or 10 years' time."

THE RISE AND RISE OF THE STAGE HUNTER

By William Fotheringham, August 27 2021

In the mid-1990s, riders who wanted to be in the winning break on a hilly stage of the Tour de France or Giro d'Italia had a fairly simple option: keep a good look-out for the Swiss pro Pascal Richard, and make sure they went where he did.

As long as they had the legs to keep at the front of the bunch in the magic hour at the start when the breaks were developing, eyesight good enough to track who was making the moves, and a clear enough head amidst the lactate fog to make the split-second decision to follow.

Richard was an early example of the stage hunter, a particular type of bike racer and a breed that has become increasingly significant in the last two decades. Back then, he landed six stage wins at the Giro and Tour, as well as another 10 stages at races which now have an important slot in the WorldTour: Paris-Nice, Tirreno, Romandie, the Tour of Switzerland.

It's crucial to point out that the Swiss wasn't JUST a rider who targeted stage wins in major races. His skill set, climbing, explosiveness and tactical acumen, enabled him to win the Olympic Games road race, Liège-Bastogne-Liège and the Giro di Lombardia, but he raced these in the usual Classic style, waiting for the final hour. Where he was ahead of his time was in his approach to the stage races: the overall was never a priority, instead he and the DS who managed him for the best years of his career, Giancarlo Ferretti, would have their eyes on certain targeted stages.

This sounds very routine to the 21st century follower of cycling, but a quarter of a century ago, things were a bit different. Nowadays, at the Vuelta and the Giro, the hilly stages that the stage hunters circle in the route book are far more common, to the extent that they equal or outnumber either pure mountain stages or sprint stages. These days, organisers seek out the crazily steep climbs that create opportunities for the opportunists: back then, at the Tour de France at least, hilly stages tended to be "transition" days that happened to be in the route because they conveniently took the riders from A to B.

There's been a change, but it's a subtle one. Teams have always gone to stage races aspiring to win stages, they've just rarely done it as methodically, or as overtly, or as well as certain teams seem to do right now. Ferretti's MG Technogym were an exception back then with their philosophy of simply raising hell in the first hour and getting riders in the move: nowadays, the way they rode has echoes in what we see on an almost daily basis at the Vuelta or Giro from teams like DSM or EF Education.

The change has come for good reasons. All three Grand Tours have become incredibly significant, not just the Tour. At the same time, it's getting harder and harder for even WorldTour teams to win a Grand Tour overall. Of the last 12 Grand Tours, only two have gone to a rider outside Sky/Ineos, Jumbo and UAE. This is partly economics: Team Sky and now Ineos, Jumbo and UAE have changed the game to the extent that attempting to put together a WorldTour team that is truly going to contend for overall victory is simply beyond the means of many teams.

It's also a risky way to allocate budget. Why invest the bulk of what you've got in one or two riders and a trail of high-class domestiques when a minor lurgy or a major crash can make the investment void? In similar vein, why buy up one sprinter and build a lead-out train around them, when the risk is similar – as Lotto-Soudal will attest after Caleb Ewan's crash this year – and when there are fewer sprint stages in any case.

Better to buy up as many possible stage winners as you can. (There's an alternative here, which is the Quickstep answer:

have the strongest Classics team on the block, and alongside that, construct a lead-out train and invest annually in several sprinters who are just behind the very best in current results and market value). There's a final factor: organisers have increasingly followed the example of Christian Prudhomme at the Tour, and tried to build routes which encourage attacking racing. Aided by Spanish and Italian terrain, the Vuelta and Giro have run with this principle, such that a bunch sprint stage seems like an aberration.

Hence (drum roll) the rise of the stage hunter, one of the best examples in recent years being Steve Cummings in his heyday of 2015-16. Cummings wasn't a Classic rider who won stages in Grand Tours and WorldTour races, he was a stage race specialist who targeted his days like a sniper looking down his telescopic sights. And it paid dividends: five major stage wins in two years, plus the overall at the Tour of Britain (won in stage hunter style, by targeting one particularly hard day).

Stage hunting isn't just about going to a race with a possible stage winner and hoping for the best. There have been plenty of Sergio Léone references in this year's Vuelta, what with stages going close to his Spaghetti Western film sets; the best stage hunters remind me of his fictional bounty hunters. It's about how efficiently, inventively and ruthlessly you go about using the resources you have and the opportunities that present themselves. Deceuninck-Quickstep are in a class of their own, but alongside them, two teams in particular are following the stage hunter route: EF Education, and DSM.

Look back to last year's Tour de France and you have to admire the tactical brilliance with which the German team, then Sunweb, took their stages with Søren Kragh Andersen and Marc Hirschi. Similarly, this year's Vuelta, with Michael Storer and Romain Bardet. As for EF, think back to the Giro and Alberto Bettiol, and last year's Tour and Dani Martínez. Plus the consummate stage hunter of the moment: Magnus Cort Nielsen, who is doing the long-range stuff with consummate brilliance, and grabbing openings when they come his way. Best of all, there are at least five more Vuelta stages that suit the likes of Storer and MCN.

NO WINS FOR SPAIN BUT REASONS FOR OPTIMISM

By Peter Cossins, September 4, 2021

Unless Enric Mas can channel the spirit, verve and finishing power of his Movistar teammate and four-time Liège-Bastogne-Liège winner Alejandro Valverde and win Saturday's penultimate, Liège-style stage of the Vuelta a España around the Galician town of Mos, it looks certain that the race will end without a home rider tasting victory for the first time since 1996.

Back then, when the Italians were winning stages for fun and Swiss trio Tony Rominger, Alex Zülle and Laurent Dufaux filled the podium, Spain's winless Vuelta was a blip, as the country's cycling scene was in rude health. Although Spanish fans had just waved a surprise *adios* to five-time Tour de France champion Miguel Induráin, who quit the race and, it soon turned out, the sport on the road to Lagos de Covadonga, there was plenty of reason for optimism.

In ONCE, Banesto and Kelme, Spain had three very competitive teams, while Euskadi were on the way up too. The national calendar was busy as well. Almost every region had its own week-long stage, some had two or three, while the amateur/under-23 scene was vibrant, especially in the Basque Country, where almost every budding Spanish talent had to go and prove themselves if they wanted to have a chance of stepping up to the pro ranks.

On the face of it, the situation now seems very different, less rosy. Spain has just a single WorldTour team, Movistar keeping alive the flame lit by Reynolds in the 1980s and carried subsequently by the likes of Banesto and Caisse d'Épargne. The Spanish calendar has been decimated, and other sports have become more popular among the younger generation, which has slowed the conveyor belt of talent into the peloton.

The fact that no Spanish rider has won a stage at any of the Grand Tours this year, the first time this has happened, adds to the sense that Spanish cycling is in the doldrums. This feeling is compounded by the fact that many of the country's leading riders are either in or approaching the veteran category, Valverde most obviously, but also Luis León Sánchez, the Izagirre brothers, Pello Bilbao and Mikel Landa.

However, all that said, I'm ending this Vuelta with a sense of real optimism for Spanish cycling. Enric Mas is one significant reason for that. Even if he doesn't manage to hang on to second place on GC over the final weekend, he looks a better, more competitive, more threatening Grand Tour racer than he was when he finished runner-up to Simon Yates in the 2018 edition. Like every other rider who has come up against the doubled-headed Slovenian steamroller of Primož Roglič and Tadej Pogačar in the last couple of years, he's been second best. But he's been aggressive, judged his efforts well and looks much more like a potential Grand Tour winner.

Further down the standings, Trek-Segafredo's Juan Pedro López has fought his way up to the fringes of the top 10 in only his second Grand Tour. Clearly a very talented climber, at 24 he's another good prospect. The three pro conti teams, Burgos-BH, Caja Rural and Euskaltel-Euskadi, have distinguished themselves too.

But the biggest reason for Spanish optimism during the past three weeks has been triggered not by events at the Vuelta, but on French roads at the Tour de l'Avenir. On the final stage, Ineos Grenadier Carlos Rodríguez produced a stunning ride to the Col du Petit Saint-Bernard that almost resulted in him taking the stage and the overall title in one great coup. Ultimately, he finished seven seconds down on Norwegian winner Tobias

Johannessen. Fourth at the Ruta del Sol, consistent in his support for his leaders at the Critérium du Dauphiné and only 20 years old, he's definitely one to keep an eye on, starting this week at the Tour of Britain. *[At the British Tour, Rodríguez would prove to be a strong worker as Ethan Hayter tried and narrowly failed to win overall]*

Then there's *el fenómeno*, Juan Ayuso, born in Barcelona, brought up in Atlanta (USA) and Xàbia (Alicante) and signed by UAE Team Emirate until the end of 2025. Set to turn 19 in the middle of this month, he looks more rounded than climbing specialist Rodríguez and is already being hailed as Spain's next big Grand Tour prospect.

Winner of the Spanish junior road title at 16, he retained it the following year and doubled up in the time trial. Riding for the Italian Colpack-Ballan U23 team, he finished top 10 at the Settimana Coppi e Bartali won by Jonas Vingegaard in March, and has subsequently stormed through the under-23 calendar, where the highlight was his victory in the Baby Giro, his final race for Colpack. Winner of three stages, he finished the race almost three minutes clear of runner-up Johannessen, taking the points, mountains and youth classification for good measure. Outsprinted by Luis León Sánchez for the win at the GP Ordizia in late July, he was then a top 20 finisher on his WorldTour debut at the San Sebastian Classic. Unfortunately, a crash on the fourth stage of the Tour de l'Avenir prevented a reprise with his Baby Giro battle with Johannessen and of the opportunity to see what havoc he might have wreaked in the mountains with Spain teammate Rodríguez. Having followed the growing trend and made the jump from the junior ranks straight into the WorldTour, Ayuso's next target is the European Under-23 Championships in Trento later this month.

Ultimately, while Spain may have missed out in this Vuelta and is facing the prospect of seeing some of its standard-bearers retire, Enric Mas doesn't look like he'll be out there on his own for long. Reinforcements are coming, and fast!

THE 2021 VUELTA: THE POWER OF THREE

By William Fotheringham, September 5 2021

Primož Roglič *and the hat-trick*

It's the big stat of this Vuelta: Roglič equals Tony Rominger's hat-trick of Vuelta wins, and does so while winning four stages. There are plenty of remarkable things about the former ski-jumper's cycling career – not least that he didn't start racing until the age of 24 – but the one that intrigues me is his ability to bounce back after misfortune. It's not as if he does this once in a while; his career has a saw-tooth profile that is more Fausto Coppi than Bernard Hinault.

So last year we have the catastrophic final stage of the Tour, followed by victory at Liège and the Vuelta. This year, the disastrous finale to Paris-Nice, followed by the Tour of the Basque Country; the horrendous crash at the Tour, followed by an Olympic gold medal and the Vuelta. It's worth asking at this point how a rider can dominate the Vuelta three times – and this year's win was particularly dominant – but not win the Tour? I'd suggest three things: less pressure at the Vuelta compared to the Big Boucle, shorter, punchier climbs, and a slightly weaker field. This was an assured, confident win, summed up by the fact that he had no inhibitions about donating the leader's jersey to Intermarché, and no signs of haste in getting it back. It wasn't suspenseful in the slightest, but the anarchic nature of the rest of the race made up for that. And hats off to the three team mates who have supported Roglič in all three wins: Robert Gesink, Lennard Hofstede and Sepp Kuss.

Three stage wins for Fabio Jakobsen One of the most heartwarming stories of the season: the Dutch sprinter's return from a coma after that horrendous crash in Poland 12 months ago to stake his claim among the sprint elite once again. That's a huge tribute to his bravery, patience and capacity for hard work. But his comeback, and Mark Cavendish's, jointly reflect an intriguing bigger picture, with no sprinter dominant this year, although Cav's four Tour stage wins are a bigger total than any other sprinter has achieved in Grand Tours in 2021. None for Sam Bennett, only two for Caleb Ewan – who'd have expected that at the start of the season?

Three stage wins for Magnus Cort Nielsen The Dane's trio of stages were a triumph for team work at EF – lest we forget, they lost their GC rider Hugh Carthy early on – and reflect his all-round prowess: on the summit finish at Cullera he escaped solo and narrowly eluded Roglič; at Córdoba, he outwitted UAE and Matteo Trentin, while his win from the break at Monforte de Lemnos belonged as much to his team mate Lawson Craddock.

Three leaders at the Team Ineos "Trident" This wasn't an outright disaster for Ineos, but given their massive budget, the expectations around them, and their brave words about racing in a more enterprising way, it's not great to field three potential winners in Richard Carapaz, Egan Bernal and Adam Yates, and come away with so little, apart from the Bernal break en route to Lagos de Covadonga which ultimately gained nothing. And coming after a below-par Tour, it hardly looks like progress.

Three successful Grand Tours for Alpecin-Fenix After a good Giro and a fantastic Tour, a solid Vuelta thanks to Jasper Philipsen's brace of stage wins. Evidence that you don't need to be WorldTour to win races, and you don't just have to rely on an iconic leader named van der Poel. Going back to pre-season predictions, did anyone expect them to win sprint stages at all three Grand Tours this year?

Three reasons for Intermarché-Wanty Goubert to smile Although they lost their GC leader Louis Meintjes to a late crash, this was another Grand Tour that marked progress for the new kids in the WorldTour, with Rein Taaramäe's stage win and brief spell in the leader's jersey followed by Odd Christian Eiking's longer sojourn in red. It's always interesting to see what happens when a team get a leader's jersey to defend, and at this point the Belgian underdogs took on a new dimension and began racing like a GC team.

Three stage wins for Team DSM Heartening to see Romain Bardet back racing hard, and yet another Australian climbing revelation for the German team, with Michael Storer following Jai Hindley last year. The Vuelta was originally moved to its end of season slot to provide teams with a chance for redemption after the Tour and Giro, and DSM grabbed the chance. Three stage wins and the King of the Mountains was a more than decent return after a disastrous Tour de France. But between Magnus Cort Nielsen, Roglič, Jakobsen and DSM there wasn't a great deal left for the other teams.

Three best stage finishes Stage 20 – Clément Champoussin, Castro de Herville. A coup de theatre by an underdog, all it wanted was for the Frenchman to thumb his nose at the GC riders as they foxed and feinted at the race's final summit finish.

Stage 19 – Magnus Cort Nielsen, Monforte de Lemos. You feel for the chasing teams, DSM and especially BikeExchange, but you cheer for the seven man break as no one misses a turn and Lawson Craddock gives his all. And you know MCN is going to win from the moment the chasers crack.

Stage 13 – Florian Sénéchal, Villanueva della Serena. The world's best lead-out team gets it horribly wrong, with designated sprinter Fabio Jakobsen falling to bits as Josef Černy rips the string to shreds. And then DQS somehow get it back together with Sénéchal, although you can't help thinking: if the Frenchman had come second (that unlucky Matteo Trentin the nearly man again) what would the debrief have been like? The madness and the anarchy of the Vuelta in three crazy kilometres.

Chapter Eight: The Mathematician, the New Merckx and the Struggles of a Multiple Tour Winner

ANNA HENDERSON: JUMBO-VISMA'S RISING STAR

By Nick Bull, May 5 2021

Anna Henderson may only be 22, and in her first full season of top-level racing, but she's already fully aware about what it means to respect races. After her breakaway attempt at Flèche Wallonne came to an end on the Côte d'Ereffe, a little over 20 kilometres from the finish, not even the race's nasty finale and her impending debut at Liège-Bastogne-Liège was going to stop the British rider from packing, let alone doing something frowned upon even more by fans of the sport.

"The Mûr de Huy does not lie," she said. "I'm going to admit it: I nearly had to walk up the climb the second time round. I was that done, but my pride stopped me from getting off my bike. To put it in perspective, a group caught me at the bottom of the Mûr and they put two minutes into me by the top. That's how slowly I went up it!"

Despite her final kilometre struggles, it was a ride that generated great pride for Henderson. She said: "Making it as far as I did was really cool. I was intrigued to see how I'd cope on the climbs – they just keep on coming in that race. Getting in the breakaway was a real experience, getting to within 20 kilometres of the finish even more so."

Having only experienced 10 racing days last year, a season that ended after the world championships owing to a positive

COVID diagnosis, Henderson's 2021 to date suggests how highly-rated she is by Team Jumbo-Visma's management as they take on their debut season. The Briton raced Het Nieuwsblad, Le Samyn, Nokere Koerse, Gent, Flanders and then the two Belgian races that feature in Ardennes week. She placed 20th at Omloop and 24th at the Ronde, her best results in this block.

"I keep surprising myself in races," she said. "Every time I've managed to follow the front group I've thought 'oh, OK, I've got some good shape here!' Flanders was incredible, although I felt like I'd been hit by a bus the next day. I was hoping to get a little bit further than the Kwaremont, but it wasn't bad for a first attempt. What you experience on the climbs there is just another level of hard. You suffer throughout. It seems like everybody pushes themselves to suffer a few percent more at Flanders than, say, at Nieuwsblad."

A short pause is then followed up: "But I'm definitely looking forward to it again next year! I think the Classics are definitely where my strengths lie so I've enjoyed the first part of this season so much. The team have given me the opportunity to play different roles and expand my knowledge of top-level racing. I think I'd be foolish not to pursue targeting these races again in 2022."

It feels quite remarkable that Henderson is only 22, given how established she was on the British racing scene. A former national circuit race champion, Henderson won four rounds across two editions of the Tour Series (including two solo, one from a bunch sprint) in 2018 and 2019. However, signs that she was far more than an excellent criterium rider were visible before this spring. She placed second behind Canyon SRAM's Alice Barnes in the 2019 British road race championships in Norfolk, then finished in the same group as her current team-mate Marianne Vos, Lizzie Deignan, Kasia Niewiadoma and other big names in the gruelling world championship road race in Yorkshire three months later.

Henderson managed just six racing days – all in Australia – at the start of 2020 before her debut pro season with Team Sunweb was interrupted by the pandemic. Despite being regarded for her bike handling skills during her time racing domestically, she used the time to improve what she saw as her biggest weakness. "I really struggled with my descending at the start," she admitted. "People tried telling me I'd be great at descending because I could corner well in the Tour Series."

Her downhill struggles are largely attributable to Henderson's cycling background: she only picked up the sport aged 17, having been a junior British skiing champion. (Avoiding any comparison to fellow Jumbo-Visma rider Primož Roglič here is advisable because, as Henderson says, "he was jumping, I was staying on the snow".)

Her first introduction to cycling came when she unsuccessfully applied to join British Cycling's Academy Sprint Programme, before she switched her attention to road racing. Henderson said: "Because I came in late to cycling, nobody ever really taught me how to descend until recently. I had to put a lot of work in, particularly last year. That's the beauty of the outdoors and cycling: it's free. I didn't need to go to a gym, swimming pool or training centre to work on my skills, so I didn't miss out during lockdown. I think you get the same rush when you really nail a turn, that doesn't change between the two sports. Technically, they're both hard skills, there's some crossover, but after a while I got there!"

Henderson says work on "short, technical descents" in and around the Chilterns, where she lives when she's back in the UK, as well as training camps in Austria and Spain helped her significantly. Her work has already paid off: at last year's La

Course, she placed herself in the race's breakaway group, one that formed coming off the Aspremont climb first time around. "As a team, we just wanted to be the first onto the descent, solely to stay safe," she recalled. "Before I knew it, there were a few of us away. The fact it was La Course added a little bit of extra spice!" Her presence up front in the back end of Flèche was a similar story: "completely unplanned," she admitted. "I was just following the wheels on a descent and we got a gap. It was cool to put pressure on the teams that missed it, the likes of SDWorx and Liv Racing. It was fun to play that game."

Given how upbeat and positive Henderson has always been whenever I've spoken to her, that she says she has yet to feel overawed while racing this season is of little surprise. "I mean, I definitely knew I was on the Côte d'Ereffe at Flèche when the radio said 'Anna is dropping, Anna is dropping'," she joked. "When I'm racing, I don't really think about what's happening or where I am. There's no pinching myself going on." I believe this is what should be called the Vos effect; the spreading of an unwavering focus by an accomplished leader to all of those around her.

Henderson has already played noted roles in her team-mate's victory at Ghent-Wevelgem, as well as Vos' third-place finish at the GP Oetingen. "You can see the wealth of knowledge and experience she has," said Henderson. "You ask her 'how does this race go, what happens here, where I do need to be in the peloton and when?' and then you realise that she's won it in the past. It's really amazing to be able to tap in to that. She's really calm, really collected. I'd love to be in a position where I have that knowledge in a few years' time."

Come 2022, one thing Henderson should have to her name is an undergraduate degree in Sport and Exercise Science from the University of Birmingham. Impressively, she's managing to split her time between this and her cycling career, something

Henderson described as being "classic me". She added: "Most of the time it's been fine, but there have been a couple of moments when there's a big race on a Sunday and then I've got a deadline on the Monday and I think 'oh, this is going to be fun!' But taking five years to do a three-year course isn't so bad in the end, right?" As Henderson's ride up the Mûr de Huy second time around at Flèche Wallonne showed, it's all about making it to the finish line. How you get there isn't nearly as important.

[Henderson would go on to put in a superbly strong ride at the world championships in Leuven in late September, suggesting she has the power to replace Lizzie Deignan as GB team leader in the future]

REMCO AND THE WEIGHT OF EXPECTATION

By Nick Bull, May 28 2021

"I've often felt that people have no regard for athletes' mental health and this rings true whenever I see a press conference or partake in one. We're often sat there and asked questions that we've been asked multiple times before or asked questions that bring doubt into our minds and I'm just not going to subject myself to people that doubt me." **Naomi Osaka, 26 May 2021**

"We knew that the Giro could go in many different directions for me…" **Remco Evenepoel, 24 May 2021**

A single Instagram post from tennis star and reigning US Open and Australian Open champion Osaka this week reignited the ongoing conversation about the mental health of professional athletes.

By declaring that she won't attend any of her media obligations at the forthcoming French Open, Osaka acknowledged that she will be fined, potentially as much as $20,000 each time. "I believe that the whole situation is kicking a person while they're down and I don't understand the reasoning behind," she wrote. Her critics will claim that facing the press and being scrutinised is part of being a professional athlete. Supporters will say that only her performances, not her words, need to be analysed.

Based on the criticism he received from Eddy and Axel Merckx since the start of the Giro, Osaka's words wouldn't have been out of place had they come from Remco Evenepoel. "I just want to say: Remco will still have to improve in many areas to win a Grand Tour," Eddy Merckx wrote in his daily Giro column for *Het Nieuwsblad*. "I think that he underestimated the Giro. There's nothing wrong with that. Of course he's talented but the road is still long. Sometimes he seems to think he's already made it."

The idea that Evenepoel was going to be a major player in this year's Giro – his first Grand Tour, remember – is a reflection of the burden placed upon the 21-year-old. While some riders *have* been successful in their first three-week race, the Belgian started the Giro off the back of just 11 racing days since March 2019, the last of which ended with the frightening sight of him plunging over a bridge at Il Lombardia last August. He was only cleared to resume training in early February. Considering the challenging route, inclement weather conditions and a GC field featuring Egan Bernal, Simon Yates, Aleksandr Vlasov and Romain Bardet, that he sat seventh overall after 15 stages was nothing short of impressive. The same can be said of his fourth-placed finishes on Ascoli Piceno and the gravelled climb of Campo Felice. It's also worth reminding ourselves that Evenepoel came into the race acknowledging that his primary obstacle wasn't the opposition or the *parcours*. "First of all, I just want to get used to the bunch again," he said. "It's always quite tricky to ride in a bunch, for sure, during nervous stages."

Why has Merckx criticised Evenepoel so publicly? Is he actually threatened by anybody who is labelled "the next Merckx"? Forget Hannibal Lecter, we've just come across cycling's Cannibal Lecturer. Prior to turning 21, Evenepoel won the Tours of Poland, Burgos, Algarve, San Juan and Belgium, so claiming that he underestimated the Giro is a staggering accusation. "It's all part of the learning process," he said after losing 24 minutes to Bernal in Monday's stage to Cortina d'Ampezzo. "I'm taking that lesson into next year."

Admittedly, Osaka acknowledged in her Instagram post that she has a "friendly relationship with most" journalists. As somebody who will only ever ask questions as opposed to answering them, I'm fully aware that this next claim is akin to marking my own school work. Nonetheless, in Evenepoel's case, I'd say that Merckx's comments about him are far more damaging than any question directed at him in the Giro's first rest day press conference. Nor are Merckx's recent remarks the first time that he's singled out Evenepoel. "Let's not get ahead of ourselves with Remco," Merckx said last summer. "He hasn't shown anything yet. He talks a lot, but I am waiting to see the rest." The Deceuninck-Quick Step rider was incredibly gracious in response to these comments: "Eddy Merckx has the right to put someone in their place," he told *Het Nieuwsblad*. "Look at his career, there is nothing to add."

Perhaps, in hindsight, it was a mistake giving him the 91 dossard for the race (something that the team have said was a decision made by Giro organiser RCS). Making him co-leader alongside João Almeida did little to manage people's expectations, but are Deceuninck really to blame for that? The team's general manager Patrick Lefevere acknowledged this to *Het Laatste Nieuws* this week: "The only thing we could not control was the euphoria that arose in Flanders in the run-up to the Giro. But that is precisely why we, and certainly the press, do not have the right to judge Evenepoel."

I'm no fan of the over-used "I'll take it day by day" line that GC contenders robotically come out with ahead of Grand Tours, however I sensed genuine authenticity in Evenepoel's expectation-lowering comments he made pre-race. "I'll be happy if I can end this Giro without any setbacks or problems, or talking about injuries and all that stuff," he said before the race started in Turin. The Belgian reiterated doubts over his performance level on the first rest day, too. "Maybe in this press conference next week, I'll be 10th," he said. At the time, he was second overall.

Unless Bernal fades badly in this year's race between now and Sunday's time trial into Milan and concedes the *maglia rosa* to

Damiano Caruso, the gap to the last Italian winner of the Giro will extend to five years. God help the next native rider to show any GC potential in the years to come while that run continues. The sooner everybody does away with labels such as "France's next Tour de France winner" or "the new Merckx" the better.

Evenepoel is not even 18 months removed from being a teenager. He's already being subjected to a level of scrutiny that is both uncomfortable and evokes Thibaut Pinot's and Tom Dumoulin's candid comments they made about the sport earlier in the year. If the Frenchman saying "there's no fun [in cycling] any more" and Dumoulin admitting that he struggled to deal with the weight of expectation surrounding him didn't make you sit up and consider the mental health of professional riders, I'm not sure what will. So what if we don't know how good Evenepoel is going to be in Grand Tours after his Giro debut? Fans, experts and former professionals alike should embrace the intrigue, as opposed to kicking him while he's down.

FROOME HANGS ON TO GIVE BACK

By Jeremy Whittle, June 30 2021

Chris Froome's staying power has never been in doubt. Four stages after hitting the deck at high speed on the very first stage of the 2021 Tour to Landernau, he is suffering through the pain, putting a brave face on, and insisting that his comeback remains on track.

Time trial helmet removed, leaning against the barriers beyond the finish line in Laval, Israel SUN's biggest star was in reflective mood as he recovered from the Tour's first individual time trial, from Changé to Laval. If Froome was still in anything like as much pain as he had appeared to be, five days earlier, he wasn't letting on. "I've got a lot of dark bruising on my upper leg, and my chest, but I don't think I'm the only one in the peloton with aches and pains," he said. "A lot of guys have come down these last few days and looking around the peloton, I can't ever remember seeing so many injured riders. It's pretty scary."

It has been a torrid start to the Tour for Froome and his team mates. Their best-placed rider, Canadian Guillaume Boivin, was in 54th place, over six minutes off the GC pace, as the first time trial began. Froome, meanwhile, after being derailed yet again on his road back to being a contender, admitted he had been moved by Mark Cavendish's return to winning form in Fougeres. "There's a lot of emotion there," he said of Cavendish's tears on the finish line. "The pressure that is put on the guys, especially at this level. It's to be expected."

"It was amazing to see Cav do that," he said. "Everybody had written him off. The Tour is where you're measured as a professional cyclist. For Cav to have come back and won another stage at the Tour – and he'll probably go and win another one in the next few days – is just phenomenal."

Perhaps seeing his old team mate return to the pinnacle of road racing, when he – like Froome, had been seen as yesterday's man – was the inspiration Froome needed. Right now, however, the four-time winner has got a big battle on his hands, just to recover from his injuries.

"We've got the mountains coming soon, so I'm hoping I come around a little bit more before we hit them. I'm starting to feel like the side I crashed on on the first day is starting to work again now. I know I'm nowhere near the pace on today's course, it was just about getting through the day.

Asked what was his main goal, Froome responded: "To help my team mates win a stage." This, he said, was "nothing new" to him. "When I go into a race that I know I can't win myself, I'll be happy doing a job to help somebody else. For years of my career, I have had people helping me and it's nice to give back a little bit. Even though it's been really technical and dangerous racing, I am loving being back at the Tour de France. I've missed that in the last two years and it feels amazing to be back here."

CALCULATING KIESENHOFER: OUTSMARTING THE PELOTON

By Amy Jones, September 6 2021

In the wake of Anna Kiesenhofer's surprise win in Tokyo the emphasis fell not on the Austrian's extraordinary achievement, but on the failure of the Dutch squad and the rest of the peloton to realise she was up the road. After Annemiek van Vleuten crossed the line mistakenly celebrating winning the race, she and her teammates huddled together confusedly. Kiesenhofer was metres away but barely anyone congratulated her.

As confusion reigned in the aftermath of the race, the feat that the 30-year-old had just pulled off – taking Austria's first cycling Olympic gold medal since 1896 – became almost the second-tier story behind the blame game that had started amongst the rest of the riders. A lack of information and no race radios had contributed to the remaining riders thinking they were fighting for gold, but the onus was on them to be aware of Kiesenhofer's presence up the road. That the Austrian, who has considerable time trialling pedigree, was still up the road was testament to her own strength as much as the other rider's failings.

Although she came from relative obscurity, Kiesenhofer's win was no fluke. With a PhD in mathematics, she knew exactly what she was doing going into the race, she had calculated it perfectly. In a since-deleted Tweet, Kiesenhofer detailed her scientific approach to the race, revealing her foray into heat acclimation training in preparation for the high temperatures in Tokyo. Her experience against the clock also stood her in good stead to gauge the gap she had versus the effort she would be able to sustain to the line. For some, the fact that a so-called 'amateur' rider managed to out-fox a peloton of pros besmirched the image of women's cycling as a serious sport. The reality is, however, that this wasn't

Kiesenhofer's first rodeo, nor is she by any means a rookie in the sport. After a successful 2016 season as an amateur racing on a Spanish team – which included winning the overall Spanish national series and taking a stage win on Mont Ventoux at the Tour Cycliste Féminin International de l'Ardèche – Kiesenhofer signed for Lotto-Soudal for 2017.

The fact that the 27 year old's season on the UCI squad stuttered to a halt in April belies her physical capabilities. What she experienced that season was a fear of riding in the peloton and an aversion to the structure of teams that led to her realising that the pro life was, in fact, not for her.

What makes Kiesenhofer's story so compelling is both the extraordinary circumstances of her win, and also her outsider's attitude to the sport in which she is now Olympic Champion. While many in her position would be relishing the influx of contract and sponsorship offers, Kiesenhofer has no desire to ride professionally again or take on paid partnerships at random. She told *VeloNews*: "I will not start advertising a pair of socks for a few hundred bucks, it's not worth it. So, I have to focus on the big things."

Equally, Kiesenhofer does not have any interest in becoming a professional cyclist again owing to her nervousness in the bunch. Such is her aversion to riding in the peloton that it spawned the break which delivered her Olympic win. Kiesenhofer spent the race off the front of the peloton from kilometre zero after initiating the move that subsequently launched her winning break, simply because she did not want to be in the peloton.

Racing for a living used to be her dream, but since realising her own mental limitations she has the self-awareness to know that pro life is not for her, "I don't see myself in a pro team and just riding and doing what I'm scared of and riding in the bunch," she told *VeloNews*. Her lack of interest in pro racing has as much to do with her nerves as her anti-authoritarian attiude. In the same interview she had this advice for young riders entering the sport: "I just wanted to say, you shouldn't trust them too much. You should continue thinking for yourself and being critical. Listening to people but being critical and not just believing everything."

Kiesenhofer's unorthodox route to Olympic gold and her rejection of certain mores of the sport make for a compelling narrative that can only benefit women's cycling. The story of her tenacity transcended the sport and gave it publicity in new ways. The fact that she is technically an amateur rider harks back to the original roots of the Olympic Games wherein only amateur athletes were able to compete until the middle of the 20th century.

Many younger riders could learn from Kiesenhofer's attitude to the sport, but the lesson from the postdoctoral fellow in mathematics at the École Polytechnique Fédérale de Lausanne for the rest of the peloton is: when it comes to calculating a time gap, you can count on a mathematician to get it right.

MAGICIAN MARTIN MOVES ON

By William Fotheringham, September 4 2021

Suddenly, there is a touch of autumn in the air. The Vuelta is all but over – thrilling to the last with yet another wild and woolly stage on Friday won by Magnus Cort Nielsen – the Tour of Britain is on us, the World's are just round the corner, after which it's Paris-Roubaix, the Tour of Lombardy and a straight run through to Christmas. There will be the usual run of retirements, which began last Friday with Kirsten Wild's Covid-enforced career ending, and which continued on the Vuelta's penultimate stage with news that Dan Martin will hang up his wheels at the end of this season.

I will miss Martin in 2022. He's a predictably unpredictable bike racer who has made a career out of making things happen. The first time I saw him in action was at the Tour of Britain in 2010, when he made a massive effort to win the stage over the Quantock hills and into Glastonbury. It didn't work out, but no one minded; most of those present were trying to figure out how the new kids on the block, Team Sky, and their hugely expensive leader Bradley Wiggins, had contrived to lose the stage to a little known Italian, Marco Frapporti.

Martin was already in his third year as a pro, and it's one measure of how long the Irishman has been around that he pre-dates the entire Sky/Ineos era. Another is to check out the line-up of the 2010 Garmin-Transitions team (who can forget the slogan Always the Right Protection for Your Eyes?): Martin is, by my estimate, the last man standing. He's never been prolific, but he's had the knack of winning memorably, winning big, and winning races prestigious enough to forge a career to be proud of.

Over the years, Jonathan Vaughters's teams have built a reputation for a buccaneering approach to racing, often targeting stage wins as well as or instead of GC; we've seen it to great effect in this Vuelta with Cort Nielsen. Martin, I'd argue, played a key role in forging that style in his eight seasons at the team. You could point to his pedigree – the nephew of 1987 Tour winner Stephen Roche, the son of Milk Race stalwart Neil Martin – but it's far more than genetics.

A week ago I wrote about the breed of bike racers that I think of as stage hunters, and Martin was one of that crew. He was good enough to finish in the top 10 of a Grand Tour – he managed six top 10s with a best of fourth in last year's Vuelta – but his stage wins stick in my mind more: the first at the Tour de France in 2013 at the end of an absolutely brutal stage through the Pyrenees, last year's at the Vuelta when he outsprinted the two strongest riders in the race, Primož Roglič and Richard Carapaz, and this year's at the Giro, when he had the legs and the guts to hold off the GC group on the Sega di Ala finish.

In 2017, Martin might have made the podium in the Tour, but for a couple of pieces of ill fortune. He explained his approach to racing to me towards the end of the race. "It's all on circumstance, although I'm a lot more calculating this year. Last year I attacked quite recklessly sometimes. I'm using attacks with more purpose this time," he said. "You need to have an idea of what's going to happen but, if you have a plan in your head before the start, then you possibly miss opportunities that arise." Sometimes, he has had the famed ill luck of the Irish: at Liège-Bastogne-Liège in 2014 he hit a patch of oil when poised to win for the second year running. In Belfast later that year, there was the slippery drain cover in the Giro's team time trial opener, that left him with a broken collar bone.

There have been two jewels of Classic wins; 2013 at Liège and 2014 in Lombardy, both born of superb tactical instincts; positioning and timing 100% accurate, so too the ability to identify the key moment to make the move. Either could be shown to young riders as textbook examples of how to win a bike race when you are not necessarily the fastest or the most powerful.

In 2014, Martin told me: "I don't think I've ever been the strongest rider in a race but I've won because I had to learn how to beat guys tactically when I was younger rather than just using horsepower. David Millar said to me that I am an actual bike racer and that's rare these days. A lot of young riders ride on their power figures. I don't even have a power meter on my bike. I never look at power, never train by power. I race a lot on instinct and feeling." How not to admire a 21st century bike racer who rode and won with such a credo?

Chapter Nine: End of Season

TIMELINE

September 12: Wout van Aert clinches Tour of Britain victory in the final metres of the final stage after taking four of the eight stages

September 19: Filippo Ganna defends his world time trial title in Bruges from Van Aert and Remco Evenepoel

September 20: Ellen van Dijk crushes Marlen Reusser and Annemiek van Vleuten to take the women's world time trial title, eight years after her first rainbow jersey

September 22: Tony Martin rides his final race, and wins the world mixed relay title for Germany along with Lisa Klein, Niklas Arndt, Lisa Brennauer, Mieke Kröger and Max Walscheid

September 25: Elisa Balsamo springs a surprise in the elite women's road World's, outsprinting Marianne Vos and Katarzyna Niewadoma and a select group of 14. In the final race of her career, Anna van der Breggen finishes 89th, 9min 30 back

September 26: Julian Alaphilippe defends the men's world title – the first Frenchman to do so – after a late solo attack. Dylan van Baarle leads in Michael Valgren for the other medals from a chase group of four

September 30: Joss Lowden of Drops-Le Col breaks the women's Hour Record at the velodrome in Grenchen, Switzerland with a distance of 48.406km

October 2: Lizzie Deignan wins the first women's Paris-Roubaix from Vos, after an 82-kilometre solo break taking in all the cobbled sections. It is the first muddy "Hell of the North" since 2002

October 3: after more overnight rain making for the worst conditions since 1994, the men's race goes to Sonny Colbrelli

who outsprints the surprise of the day, young Belgian Florian Vermeersch – a survivor of the early escape – and Mathieu van der Poel
October 4: Nicolas Roche retires after a professional career lasting 17 years and encompassing 1,270 race days
October 9: Il Lombardia is won by Tadej Pogacar, the first rider to land Liège-Tour de France-Lombardy since Eddy Merckx in 1972
October 10: Former professional racer and television presenter Marion Rousse is named race director of the Tour de France Femmes; Arnaud Démare lands Paris-Tours, the first French victory in this Classic since 2006
October 14: The inaugural Tour de France Femmes route is confirmed, with a start on the Champs Elysées and stages across north-eastern France; the final weekend's racing in the Vosges culminates in a stage finish at La Planche des Belles Filles. The men's race returns to old Alpine stamping grounds such as the Galibier and l'Alpe d'Huez with an early stage over the Roubaix cobbles.

DENYING THE DUTCH

By Amy Jones, September 26 2021

Much as the narrative after the women's road race at the Olympic games detracted from a stunning win by Anna Kiesenhofer and focused on the Dutch team's loss, one of the main talking points to come out of the road race in Flanders was how the Dutch let yet another race that looked to be theirs in the bag go to another nation.

After years of speculation going into every major championship over how the Dutch might crumble under the pressure of having a team full of favourites, the 2021 season seems to have finally caught up with them. Until now, they have gone on to prove any doubters wrong, taking six of the previous 10 world road race titles and the 2012 and 2016 Olympic Games. Now, however, both the Tokyo road race and the world championships have shown that their strength in numbers might be less of a blessing than a curse after all.

Starting the race with eight of the peloton's best riders seems like a good way to go into a world championships, but on this occasion it seemed to work against the Dutch squad. Defending champion Anna van der Breggen did what she could in her final race as a professional but barely made it into the second group on the road having been way off her usual mark of late.

Demi Vollering – who went to Flanders as a pre-race favourite thanks to her performances this season and her strong kick – suffered mechanicals early on and received little in the way of help from her team to get back into the race. Annemiek van Vleuten and Ellen van Dijk made a good show of attacking and countering each other in the final few laps, but bizarrely also chased one another down on multiple occasions.

Van Dijk claimed that the plan was to keep attacking until 4km to go and if that wasn't to succeed they would lead out Vos for the finish: "That's where we failed," she said. "The lead-out wasn't good enough. Now she had to close a gap. If she didn't have to close that gap then it might've turned out differently. I saw it happening at 600 metres and knew it wasn't good. We weren't grouped together as we should've been at that point. We lacked the numbers there and that might've been because of all the attacks we did."

After losing the sprint against the 23-year-old Italian, Marianne Vos was in tears at the finish, clearly unhappy with the result. It was her sixth silver medal at the world championships, having been denied by Italians on five occasions with Marta Bastianelli in 2007, Tatiana Guderzo in 2009, and Giorgia Bronzini in 2010 and 2011.

In stark contrast, however, after the race, Vos said in a press conference: "That went well. We were never really out of contention. Elisa was just faster on the line, then you have to be happy with silver." Which seems like more of a concession to Balsamo's ride than praise of her team's tactics.

Indeed, regardless of any failings from the Dutch, Balsamo's sprint was perfectly executed after a consummate lead out from team mate Elisa Longo Borghini. The Italian team had their tactics perfectly lined up in the final laps of the Leuven circuit with Maria Giulia Confalonieri getting herself into all the right moves and Longo Borghini keeping things under control. Meanwhile, the Dutch team were busy chasing attacking with no clear intent.

The race in Flanders looked like it was for the Netherlands to lose; they did so, but to a more than deserving winner. It remains to be seen whether Balsamo's win over Vos marks a changing of the guard in the women's peloton or not, (the Dutchwoman can be expected to continue to win as long as she pins on a number) but the rainbow jersey will almost certainly be visible at the sharp end of races next season.

TIMING PLUS INSTINCT EQUALS JUJU

By Jeremy Whittle, September 27 2021

In the end, it was all about timing and Julian Alaphilippe's proved to be perfect. The former Tour de France yellow jersey wearer, winner of the 2020 World Championships Road Race in Italy, showed his attacking qualities once again on the final circuit of the 2021 men's road race in Belgium, with another lone win.

Back-to-back wins by the Frenchman in the World Championships are proof of his durability, continuing ambition and also his racing instincts. With all eyes on Wout van Aert, Alaphilippe's opportunism proved irresistible. He is now the eighth Frenchman to win the World title and the first to claim it twice, taking the rainbow jersey first in Imola, last autumn, and then again, in Leuven.

Appropriately, Alaphilippe's second solo success came in Belgium, also location of one of his biggest disappointments as world champion when he collided catastrophically with a motorbike, while racing in the winning break in last year's Ronde. This time however, even the few unruly Belgians, tossing beer and insults in his path as he rode clear to another memorable victory, could not deter him from sealing a spectacular win. In many ways, this was an unexpected success, even for Alaphilippe himself who admitted afterwards that he had "never imagined I'd be leaving with the rainbow jersey."

And yes, given his recent form, van Aert had been everybody's pick. Alaphilippe, well, he always has a go, sometimes it works out, but really how often in the last year or so did he follow through and take the win? That perspective however ignores the fact that he is an athlete made for the biggest of stages.

Over the past year, he has been among the most watchable

rainbow jersey wearers and remains among the most charismatic and unpredictable riders in the peloton. Look no further than a week after his success in Imola. With Liège-Bastogne-Liège seemingly won, he lifted his arms too soon and ceded victory to a surprised Primož Roglič. That embarrassment was short-lived though, and a week later he took victory in Flèche Brabançonne, even though once again, he had lifted his arms a little too hastily. Fast forward to this year's Tour de France and, after becoming a father, he was the star of the first stage, taking the win and the first maillot jaune of the race. Yet the rest of his Tour was an uneven, mixed bag with Mark Cavendish's comeback taking both the limelight and pole position in his team and the French media even accusing Alaphilippe of attacking too freely and too often.

In the rivalry between van Aert and Matthieu van der Poel, Alaphilippe has sometimes – as at last year's Ronde – been the gooseberry. In Flanders, however the pair were reduced to onlookers as their challenges failed to materialise and Alaphilippe's racing instincts took over.

The Frenchman's guile and panache has now made him a member of a pretty exclusive club of riders who have retained their world titles. He joins Belgians Georges Ronsse, (1928 and 1929), Rik Van Steenbergen, (1956 and 1957), and Rik Van Looy, (1960 and 1961), Italian duo Gianni Bugno (1991 and 1992) and Paolo Bettini (2006 and 2007) and Slovakian Peter Sagan (2015 and 2016) as world champions with back to back wins.

Afterwards, the Frenchman acknowledged that his distinctive racing style could sometimes backfire, even if it also brought him outstanding and spectacular success.

"I take a lot of pleasure to ride like this," Alaphilippe said. "I don't want to become a robot. I want to attack, with panache.

I want to give everything to try and win and it's even more beautiful when you have the rainbow jersey on."

A MUD-SOAKED MASTERCLASS FROM LIZZIE DEIGNAN

By Amy Jones, October 3 2021

Slipping and sliding but never slowing, Lizzie Deignan all but cruised over the muddy cobbles on her way to history. The 32-year-old British rider will forever be known as the first woman to win Paris-Roubaix. To boot, she is also the first ever senior British rider, male or female, to win in the Hell of the North.*

Before the race, all eyes were on Deignan's teammate, Ellen van Dijk, who with her powerful physique – and recent track record of taking the European road title and World time trial title – looked to be in perfect position to take the victory in Roubaix. Van Dijk admitted in a pre-race press conference that she would prefer dry conditions and even cried the first time she did a course recon but that she and the cobbles had since become "friends". On the day, however, those friends turned into foes and van Dijk suffered more than one tumble on the muddy pavé.

Sat beside van Dijk in the same press conference, Deignan was keen to emphasise the Dutch rider's prospects. "Everyone else finds the cobbles very difficult, but Ellen is flying over them at the moment," she said, not once revealing any personal ambitions other than an admission that: "Personally I don't mind if it rains, I mean I might say something different if it actually does and the cobbles are like ice. But I think it scares a lot of riders and rain doesn't tend to scare me. I think obviously it will make the race pretty crazy but I think it's going to be crazy anyway."

"I think our race will be off from the start, it's not a very long race and I think from the first cobbled section I expect there to be fireworks. I don't think anybody will be hanging around and you simply can't ride over these cobbles easy. So I expect it to be full-on from the beginning," she added.

Deignan's words turned out to be prescient on all counts. The wind and rain did indeed make the race "crazy" and in it, she thrived. With 80km to go, on the first sector of pavé, Deignan found herself in front solo. "That was really not the plan. I needed to be at the front in the first cobble section to protect my leaders," she admitted after the race. "Actually today I was kind of the third rider. I looked behind after the first cobbles and I thought at least if I'm in front they have to chase me, so I just kept going."

Keep going she did, and chase as they might, what was left of the rest of the peloton could not reel the Trek-Segafredo rider back in as she appeared to ride her way almost effortlessly over some of the toughest terrain in road cycling. Once or twice, her back wheel skidded across a mud-soaked surface but Deignan stayed composed and skillfully corrected each slip-up.

Those who were hoping for the epic scenes synonymous with the men's race for over 100 years will not have been disappointed. The wet conditions made the pavé treacherous and many of the favourites came a cropper; whether crashing really has a place as part of the entertainment in bike racing is a contentious topic, but it is indeed part of the sport – particularly in a race like Roubaix.

After a second crash for van Dijk in the closing stages caused a split in the chasing group, Marianne Vos saw her opportunity to attack and was visibly emptying herself to chase down the lone leader with Deignan's teammate, Elisa Longo Borghini close behind. In the end, however, it was futile and Deignan barely ceded any time to her rivals. The three riders came into the velodrome in that order, Trek-Segafredo the clear winners on the day, even if the riders in question were not the ones we might have expected.

The enduring image of the race will perhaps be the sight of an exhausted and mud-soaked Deignan and Vos congratulating each other in the velodrome. Two long-time legends of the women's peloton in an emotional embrace, standing in one of the sports most iconic arenas.

Deignan's post-race comments convey perfectly the significance of this moment for women's cycling: "I just feel so incredibly proud. Women's cycling is at a turning point and it's part of history. I'm also proud to be part of a team that also makes history," she said. "We're so grateful to everyone behind the scenes, all the viewers watching, every fan watching is also making history. It proves there's an appetite for women's cycling and the athletes here can do one of the hardest races in the world. I'm so proud I can say I'm the first ever winner."

Only seven months to wait until the next one

**The junior men's Roubaix has been won by four Britons: Geraint Thomas, Andrew Fenn, Tom Pidcock and Lewis Askey.*

LEGENDARY FLAVOUR TO FIRST ROUBAIX WEEKEND

By Peter Cossins, October 3 2021

So there we have it, the first edition of the Paris-Roubaix weekend. Two unforgettable races in what were at times apocalyptic conditions, races where every single rider who took to the start-line will certainly have a jaw-dropping story to tell, each of those contests chock-full with incident to debate, performances that should be lauded, and, above all, of reminders of what sets bike racing apart as a spectator sport.

It did seem, though, that as Sunday morning dawned, the second half of the weekend might be a fiasco rather than a triumph. Images began to circulate on social media of the hellish conditions on almost every one of Roubaix's cobbled sector. They were best summed up by a gent stripped down to his underpants swimming front crawl in a huge puddle on the fearsome section of pavé at Mons-en-Pévèle. It seemed that the prayers of so many fans for a wet Roubaix had been answered all at once, perhaps even to the point where a cancellation or at least a diversion around some of the cobbled sectors seemed possible. Indeed, the organisers of the junior edition of Roubaix, which isn't run by ASO, opted to do precisely that by removing the Mons-en-Pévèle lido section of the route from their event that took place first thing on Sunday morning.

ASO head of cycling Christian Prudhomme quickly squashed any suggestions that there might be any changes to the elite course. As the riders gathered in the gloomy grandness of Compiègne, Prudhomme told the media: 'It's Roubaix's difficulty that makes it legendary. If a rider doesn't want to start, he doesn't have to.'

When the race got under way, it seemed a good part of the

peloton wanted to adopt Lizzie Deignan's strategy from the day before – attack early and, as a consequence, arrive first at the cobbles and be able to pick the best line through them. At that point, the rain was still teeming down, turning every road junction and roundabout into a skidpan that demanded careful navigation.

When, after 100 kilometres of racing, the lead group reached the first section of cobbles at Troisvilles, my heart went into my mouth. Racing on them was almost a lottery, the central spine of the road often the only part of it standing proud of the lake-like puddles. There were crashes aplenty, and punctures and other mechanical issues were so frequent that it was nearly impossible to keep up with which riders were in which group, a task made even more complicated by the grime that quickly accumulated on their faces and chests, concealing all means of identification. From the front, the race became two-tone and could have been from almost any era. Only from above was it possible to pick out the distinctive colours of trade teams jerseys and jackets, and establish who was where.

Two moments summed up the race's descent into something approaching chaos: 2017 Roubaix winner Greg van Avermaet looking into the lens of the TV camera on the motorbike alongside him and shaking his head with evident disgust; and Christophe Laporte bending his right leg backwards to use his shoe as a brake on his rear wheel as his discs had, it appeared, jammed up with dirt.

However, just when it looked like the course might become unrideable, the weather gods intervened once again by turning off the taps as the riders neared the most testing sections of cobbles. A combination of a strong wind and the convoy of vehicles and motorbikes ahead of the race helped to disperse much of water from the pavé. Vitally, it meant that a contest that would had been a matter of survival became a full-blooded race.

There were still spills, but the riders that were able to cope the best with the conditions started to emerge. Initially, Ineos Grenadier Gianni Moscon looked set to emulate Deignan with a long-range solo win that undoubtedly wouldn't have been welcomed with the same universal delight as the British woman's success – the Italian's big talent has been overshadowed by his ability to generate controversy, including his racist abuse of Frenchman Kévin Reza, his disqualification from the 2018 Tour after punching another French rider, Elie Gesbert, and his disqualification from Kuurne-Brussels-Kuurne last year for throwing a bike at Belgian Jens Debusschere.

However, bad luck – or was it karma? – fatally undermined Moscon's hopes. It arrived first in the form of a rear wheel puncture. After swapping to his spare bike, the Italian suddenly looked uneasy on the cobbles and went down in almost exactly the same place on the Cysoing section where Deignan had managed to hold her snaking bike upright the day before. The chasing trio of Mathieu van der Poel, Sonny Colbrelli and Florian Vermeersch didn't quite reach Moscon straight away, but soon reeled him in and left him to his personal battle on the pavé once again, now riding for fourth place rather than first.

The only thing certain about the contest between this trio was that one of them was going to be the first rider to win on their Roubaix debut since a least the 1950s – 1955 victor Jean Forestier, the oldest surviving champion, was believed to be the last debutant to win but revealed in the run-up to the race that he'd abandoned before halfway the previous year. Vermeersch, 22 and best-known hitherto for his bronze medal in the World U23 Time Trial Championship last month, appeared the most unlikely winner among the three leaders, but predicting the verdict of a sprint after 257km of racing is, cycling history has often shown, never easy. In this case, though, Colbrelli fully lived up to his reputation as a sprinter of real quality.

He leapt with surprising agility from his bike, raised it above his head, then roared with a mixture of ecstasy, relief and incomprehension, which was the fitting and wonderfully cathartic reaction to what we'd all seen over the previous six hours. Around him, riders flopped to the ground, some of them disappointed, all of them absolutely exhausted. Roubaix's difficulty had added to its legend – for the second time in two days. Prudhomme had been proved right.

AUTUMN LEAVES AND YOUTHFUL PROMISE

By Jeremy Whittle, October 10 2021

It was about an hour after Tadej Pogačar had raised the roof in Bergamo by winning the 2021 Tour of Lombardy that, over one thousand kilometres away, in the same autumnal setting sun, Alexandre Balmer sped, alone, under the kilometre to go kite in the Tour de Vendée French Cup race in western France.

The fresh-faced Swiss is 21, a couple of years younger than Pogačar, and, after 175 kilometres in the break, almost pulled off an even more remarkable coup in La Roche-sur-Yon, holding off a speeding peloton until he was swept away, with under 20 metres still to race.

It was a bitter denouement. Balmer, who had only found out the previous Wednesday that he would be riding Paris-Bourges and the Tour de Vendée, had been out on his own, fending off his pursuers, for just under 20 kilometres. He's already been prodigious in his own right, hugely successful in mountain biking and also winner of a Swiss national time trial title.

Balmer's do-or-die lone move, spectacular though it was, did not compare with Pogačar's explosion of his rivals on the climb of the Passo di Ganda, over 30 kilometres from the finish in Bergamo.

Even an elite chasing group that included Primož Roglič, Julian Alaphilippe, Alejandro Valverde and Adam Yates, could not reel in the double Tour de France winner. It was an exhibition of power, resilience and self-belief, that elevated him into a select club of Tour winners – Coppi, Merckx, Hinault – who have also won the Italian Monument in the same year.

Even better was the old-school feel to his win. When was the last time a reigning Tour de France champion actively competed in Il Lombardia with an option to win? Okay, obviously there is Vincenzo Nibali, but in the past decade, Bradley Wiggins, Chris Froome, Egan Bernal, Geraint Thomas and so on, have ridden seasons that, like the leaves, fall away as autumn looms on the horizon.

Fate, and their racing schedules, will surely bring Balmer and Pogačar together again soon enough. Both are high achieving mountain bikers and accomplished climbers and their junior and under-23 career paths shadow each other. The Swiss has maintained that he will compete in the 2024 Paris Olympics in mountain biking but says that he also dreams of racing in the Tour de France. That day drew much closer after his performance on the roads of the Vendée, despite his shattering defeat within touching distance of the finish line.

Like Pogačar, Balmer appreciates what mountain biking has given him. "It's more simple in some ways," he said in 2019. "You're the only one responsible for your performance. It's straightforward: you have to give it everything. It's less tactical."

That's a sentiment that might apply to Pogačar's racing instincts at times. His winning attack to claim his first Lombardia on Saturday echoed the violent acceleration that destroyed the opposition on the 2021 Tour de France stage to Le Grand Bornand. In both those attacks, he gave it everything and never looked back.

What about tactics? What if he fails and gets caught and then dropped? That is a scenario that never seems to occur to the self-confident Pogačar, who commits wholeheartedly to those blistering accelerations.

But there is a world of difference between their environments: Pogačar, the most highly-prized asset in the peloton and currently seen as almost invincible, has a sponsorship built around his talents and rides for possibly the most powerful of the super-teams, UAE Emirates. A wealth of future success now seems assured.

Balmer in contrast, is with Groupama FDJ, a team that rarely challenges for Grand Tour success and whose image – acknowledged even by iconic star rider Thibaut Pinot – remains that of the plucky underdog. Despite his achievements in junior and under-23 racing, you'd probably never heard of him until that heart-stopping finale in the Vendée.

While Balmer is still knocking on the door and finding his way, at just 23, Pogačar has reached the sporting firmament. It's hard to imagine his career becoming more stellar, but of course, others have been here before. Remember when Jan Ullrich, Egan Bernal and others were expected to dominate the Tour de France for years to come? There is plenty that can go wrong, as others can testify.

Who knows how many major one-day and stage races Pogačar will now win? He certainly doesn't have the boom and bust vibe that has characterised others. Anybody watching his exploit on the road to Bergamo would anticipate a long and very successful career. But we cannot be sure.

Meanwhile, Balmer's performance, quickly forgotten though it may be, only emphasised the qualities of so many young riders, even outside the World Tour, where the likes of Tom Pidcock, Tobias Foss, Mauri Vansevenant and many others are already moving towards the front rank of the peloton.

It's incredible to think that at just 23, you can already be looking over your shoulder at the younger talent coming through, but that's how rapidly some of these 20-somethings are developing. The churn of talent is accelerating, and Pogačar has to seize the day. Who knows how long it will last for him? And who knows where Balmer will be in two or three years time?

LONG AND WINDING ROAD TO DENMARK'S GRAND DÉPART

By Lars B Jørgensen, October 12 2021

Not that many will remember Alex Pedersen for his professional career as a cyclist for teams like RMO and ONCE from 1988-91, as it all came to a sudden halt due to heart problems. And although Pedersen made a brief comeback in the amateur ranks to become a world champion in 1994, his days as a rider at top level were basically gone. At the beginning of the century he was a tactically astute directeur sportif at Memory Card-Jack & Jones, a team that was to become Team CSC under the reign of Bjarne Riis. In recent years Pedersen has mainly been known as one of the key figures who has worked for years to get the Tour de France's Grand Départ in the Danish capital Copenhagen.

He is one among many, but still the most familiar face in the gallery of lobbyists from high and low. To claim that it has been a long, winding and bumpy road would be an understatement. When the Tour starts in Denmark next year the event will have been more than 25 years in the making. It's a story about endless lobbying, dreams, doping scandals and not least an everlasting love of cycling.

It all began in the town of Herning back in October 1996. The same year Bjarne Riis won the Tour de France and made history. That's the sort of thing that might make some grown men cry as well as it may make others dream big. Not least in Riis' home town. The same year Tour director Jean-Marie Leblanc sat down in Herning to discuss the possibilities of a French visit to Denmark, preferably in 2002.

However the very idea of having a Tour start as far north as Denmark seemed inconceivable. Back then, West Berlin in

1987 had stretched the limits of logistics. Starting in "rural" Denmark was even more far out so to speak. And then came the issue of doping. When Riis won the Tour in 1996 no one really seemed to know or even care, but when the Festina scandal rumbled into view two years later everyone had to. The thought of attracting a "two wheeled pharmacy" cooled the interest of the public. Doubts over cycling's credibility were even aired by the chair of the Danish Tour committee that was in dialogue with ASO.

Having followed cycling for decades from a Danish perspective one thing is clear. There are storms and there is calmness. Whether it be the success of the star studded Team CSC, team-boss Bjarne Riis's pistol-on-the-forehead doping confession in 2007 or compatriot Michael Rasmussen's controversial suspension in the yellow jersey in the same year. And then CSC winning the Tour with Carlos Sastre the year after with Riis having reestablished himself as a talismanic team leader.

However, there were still no signs of a Tour start in Denmark. In the meantime, the Tour de France had taken off from Dublin (1998), and even London (2007), following up with Yorkshire in 2014. Cycling as a whole had long been in a state of globalization.

Back in 2004 Jean-Marie Leblanc had stated that he "felt it was time to give the Danes back what they had given the Tour". Leblanc may have had the best intentions. But when Christian Prudhomme took over as race director in 2007 the Danish candidacy seemed rather dead.

Admittedly, the Tour de France is a monster of an event. Demanding in so many aspects, whether we are talking economics, infrastructure, logistics and accommodation. In comparison the road race World Championship is way more manageable. Which was proven in 2011 in Copenhagen in a week where there were enthusiastic crowds at all the events.

Mark Cavendish won gold in the men's elite road race and lost (some of) his heart to the city.

In May 2012 Herning hosted the start of the Giro d'Italia. And perhaps it dawned upon Prudhomme and ASO that Denmark could be a possibility despite challenges along the way back to France. The most defining stab at being a host country came when the Danish government along with a series of mayors proposed an official bid, announced by minister of commerce Troels Lund Povlsen in 2015. From then on Prudhomme clearly warmed to the thought of a start in Copenhagen, arguably the world's major cycling city, at a time when ASO likes to polish its green credentials.

Initially the hope was to host the Tour in either in 2019, 2020 or 2021, but the 2019 slot went to Brussels. Nice was handed the start in 2020 and it looked like time and goodwill was running out for Copenhagen and Denmark. It could be seen as one last gasp when French president Emmanuel Macron made an official visit in August 2018. He was followed by Christian Prudhomme and they handed over a maillot jaune to a visibly humbled prime minister Lars Løkke Rasmussen.

Half a year later the Tour start in Denmark for 2021 was officially confirmed, only to be hit by a combination of the Covid-19 pandemic and the postponed Euro 2020 that would collide with the Grand Départ in Copenhagen. Hence its move to 2022, and the Tour's hastily set-up Grand Départ this year in Brittany.

No one said it should come easy. Or even cheap. The cost is an estimated 12 million euros. And as always there has been a debate whether it's money well spent in terms of tourism revenue and exposure or it's just a big splash of cash. But here we are, awaiting three stages in Denmark which open with a shortish 13 km time trial in the center of Copenhagen after a team presentation in the iconic Tivoli Gardens.

Expectations are high. Danish cycling has never been in a better state. Young Jonas Vingegaard was the revelation of this summer's Tour with his second place, there is a Monument winner and a former world champion in Mads Pedersen, a seven time Grand Tour stage winner in Magnus Cort Nielsen, newly crowned world championship bronze medalist Michael Valgren, 2019 double stage winner Søren Kragh Andersen and veteran GC hope Jakob Fuglsang. It's nothing short of a cornucopia.

As director of the Grand Départ organisation 54-year-old Alex Pedersen is looking ahead. He was 25 years old when the rather crazy and wild idea of giving the Tour a Danish flavour was born among some of his constantly networking friends back in Herning. "When you're mad about the Tour de France and cycling I can see nothing bigger than this job. I'm proud and humbled by the task I've been given," Pedersen said when he was named in charge in May 2019. Big it is, that much is certain. But after so many years in the making it seems the timing is just about perfect.

THE TOUR DE FRANCE FEMMES AND THE FREEWHEELING PROGRESS OF WOMEN'S CYCLING

By Amy Jones, October 14 2021

The end of this season marks a pivotal moment for women's cycling. Steady growth has been building since the introduction of the two-tier system at the beginning of 2020 – when minimum salaries and live coverage requirements were set by the UCI. Rather than set progress back, last year's Covid-challenged season saw the introduction of new races, more television coverage, and more teams, as well as rumours of the return of a women's Tour de France.

Nowhere was the continued growth more visible than in the mud-soaked aftermath of Paris-Roubaix Femmes. Winner of the first ever edition Lizzie Deignan, perfectly expressed the significance after the race: "Women's cycling is at this turning point and today is part of history," she said. "We're so grateful to everyone behind the scenes, and every fan watching this is also making history, it's proving there's the appetite for women's cycling and the athletes can do this toughest race and I'm proud I can say I'm the first-ever winner… I'm so proud that this is where we are, that women's cycling is on the world stage."

In the wake of that seminal moment, the route for the Tour de France Femmes *avec Zwift* was announced. The effect of a Tour de France for women both on the current peloton and the future of the sport is huge. While Paris-Roubaix Femmes felt like the women were breaking through another barrier of the sport's history from which they have been excluded, for them to share in the Tour de France brand – one which transcends the sport – is an even greater step forward.

That both Paris-Roubaix and the Tour de France are owned by

ASO is indicative of just how much influence the organisation has over the sport. The power to create tangible change in women's cycling has been in ASO's hands for years, and the fact that they waited this long to use it is frustrating – but now that they have finally yielded, the effects are visible.

Already, at least three new Women's WorldTeams have been created based on the promise of the race and the publicity it will bring. Other, new stage races have been announced, including the Tours of Switzerland and Romandie. The current crop of pros will be motivated by the opportunity to showcase their strengths on the biggest platform in the sport and fight for the iconic yellow, polka-dot and green jerseys. Younger generations of hopefuls can watch that unfold, and dream of the same.

As for the route itself, it offers greater variety than some of the more cynical followers of women's racing may have given ASO credit for. Trek-Segafredo's Audrey Cordon-Ragot told *cyclingnews.com* before the announcement: "we want a stage race for everyone because we really don't have something like that on the calendar," – she will not be disappointed.

Covering 1,029 kilometres in total, the eight-day race will start on the Champs Elysées as the men's race finishes, ensuring the presence of ready-made media attention and therefore coverage. The iconic Parisian stage is not new to the women's peloton, having been the backdrop of ASO's listless nod to equality – La Course – in previous years. The inclusion of this stage serves as a reminder of the long-overdue progress that has been made since that first edition in 2014.

From there, the peloton will head east where they will tackle a combination of hilly and rolling stages that could see either sprinters or breakaways take the day. The race includes stages that traverse the white roads through the Champagne vineyards, rolling stages that could favour either breakaways or bunch finishes, and mountain days in the Vosges.

The route is back-loaded with climbing. On stage seven, the women tackle the iconic Ballon d'Alsace – which in 1905 became the first major mountain climb to feature in the men's Tour de France. The race then culminates on the Planche des Belles Filles where the yellow jersey will be decided. One glaring omission from the parcours is a time trial, which some spectators and riders would have hoped for, but racers such as Marianne Vos have said in their view it will open up the race still further.

Some have already taken umbrage with the fact that the race covers just a fraction of the country. Tour de France race director Christian Prudhomme's riposte to such criticism is: "the challenge hasn't been to create a race but to create a race that lasts, one that will be sustainable and with us in 100 years." Tired riders and staff who will not have to undergo lengthy transfers after each stage would likely take his side.

In addition to a dynamic course, ASO have promised live TV coverage of every stage and, in contrast to the outrageous discrepancy at Paris-Roubaix, a prize pot of €250,000. The winner will take home €50,000 which, while still not equal to the men's prize money, is a step forward from Prudhomme's excuse that ASO "didn't realise" how skewed the Roubaix prizes were after Deignan was awarded a paltry €1,535 to Sonny Colbrelli's €30,000.

The course may not be to the taste of all fans, but the variety of stages will give most of the top female riders the opportunity to share in this seminal moment in their sport. The first Paris-Roubaix Femmes has etched Saturday 2nd October 2021 into women's cycling history. Next year, on Sunday 30th July 2022 atop the Planche des Belles Filles, yet more history will be made as the yellow jersey winner is crowned, and women's cycling continues its ascent towards equality.

Meet the Team

OJ Borg is the *lacourseentete* podcast specialist. A broadcaster of long standing who is currently with BBC Radio Two, when not out on his bike, OJ is a long-time cycling fan who was for many years the presenter of the BBC Radio podcast *Bespoke*.

Nick Bull was drawn to cycling aged nine when the Rochester International Classic World Cup race took place on local roads in 1997. He joined *Cycling Weekly* and *Cycle Sport* as a reporter in 2011, and went on to become the magazines' news editor. A regular contributor to BBC Radio 5 Live's *BeSpoke* cycling show, he is also the PR & digital manager for the Tour of Britain and Women's Tour races. He tweets *@nickbull21*.

Peter Cossins devoured Phil Liggett's reports in his dad's newpspaper in the 70s and began work at *Cycling Weekly* as the magazine was preparing to launch *Cycle Sport*. He was *procycling* editor between 2006 and 2009 and currently specialises in writing books about the sport, having started as ghost writer on Stephen Roche's *Born to Ride*. Twice an award winner for his books, Pete currently lives with his family in the Pyrenees, with an office overlooking the Prat d'Albis climb.

William Fotheringham is lead cycling writer at *The Guardian*, having covered 26 Tours de France before retiring from front line duty in 2017. A former writer at *Cycling Weekly*, he helped launch *Cycle Sport* before founding the monthly *procycling* together with Jeremy Whittle. His best selling books include *Put Me Back on My Bike: in search of Tom Simpson* (2002), *Fallen Angel: the Passion of Fausto Coppi* (2008), and *Merckx: Half-Man, Half-Bike* (2012).

Amy Jones is a freelance writer based in Girona, Spain. She primarily covers women's cycling and is passionate about equality in sports. She contributes to *Rouleur*, *Cyclingtips* and *cyclingnews.com* and is also the editor of *Women's Cycling Weekly,* a newletter covering the week's news and content from the world of women's cycling which can be found on Substack at *mamilrepeller.substack.com*.

Matt Morris is a Shropshire based designer who started his own company in 2008 and has worked with cycling brands Orbea, Scott, Bianchi and Viner as well as a number of blue-chip companies and the Lawn Tennis Association. Like many, he was drawn to cycling by Channel Four's Tour coverage and currently enjoys thrashing his gravel bike around the lanes.

Sophie Smith has been covering cycling since 2010, beginning with regional newspaper the *Geelong Advertiser*. She joined SBS in 2011, then moved to the UK to work freelance in 2012 before returning to Melbourne where she is a regular contributor to cycling magazines and websites; she has covered the Tour de France nine times.

Jeremy Whittle began covering cycling in 1993, for *Winning* magazine, where his first assignment was interviewing a Texan upstart named Lance Armstrong. He has covered the Tour de France for 25 years, for the *Times* and currently for the *Guardian*, and joined William in launching *procycling* in 1999. His books *Bad Blood* and *Racing Through the Dark* (with David Millar) were shortlisted for the William Hill Sports Book of the Year.

SWpix.com provide *lacourseentete* with photographs; they are an independent mainly sports specific picture agency, whose live and archive imagery appears in national and regional newspapers and across many digital platforms. The swpix.com archive holds nearly a million images; for more information contact Simon Wilkinson on simon@swpix.com

Acknowledgements

We at *lacourseentete.com* would like to thank all those who have supported us this year, beginning with all our nearest and dearest who have been beside us through the ups and downs.

Additionally, our gratitude goes to:

"Founder member" Sadhbh O'Shea, for letting us use her blogs from earlier this year in this book... We wish Sadhbh all the best after her move to *Velo News* back in the spring.

Guest writers: Robyn Davidson, Lars B Jørgensen, Marco Pastonesi and Richard Williams all contributed to the website during the year – massive thanks for your support.

Brad Roe at *Peloton* magazine for giving us the opportunity to write about the rejigged calendar. Hopefully our partnerships with *Peloton* will continue to endure into a more certain future for all of us.

The team at *SWpix.com* – Simon Wilkinson, Alex Whitehead, Alex Broadway – massive thanks, your work has been vital in driving the website forward.

Those who have helped us as voices on our podcasts including the voice of Italian cycling, Marco Pastonesi. *Grazie mille ragazzi.*

Thanks too to the team at YouCaxton who made this book happen literally overnight – Bob Fowke, Robert Branton, Ella Knight.

If you've enjoyed this, why not try these...

Recent works from some of our writers

Peter Cossins
A Cyclist's Guide to the Pyrenees (*Great Northern Books*, 2021)
The Yellow Jersey (*Yellow Jersey*, 2019)
Butcher, Blacksmith, Acrobat, Sweep (*Yellow Jersey*, 2017)

William Fotheringham
The Greatest: the Times and Life of Beryl Burton (*YouCaxton*, 2019)
Sunday in Hell: Behind the Lens of the Greatest Cycling Film of All Time (*Yellow Jersey*, 2018)
The Badger: Bernard Hinault and the Fall and Rise of French Cycling (*Yellow Jersey*, 2015)
***All these titles available from* www.williamfotheringham.com**

Jeremy Whittle
One Way Ticket: Nine Lives on Two Wheels (with Jonathan Vaughters, *Quercus*, 2019)
Ventoux: Sacrifice and Suffering on the Giant of Provence (*Simon and Schuster*, 2017)
Bad Blood: the Secret Life of the Tour de France (*Yellow Jersey*, 2008)

BV - #0052 - 161121 - C5 - 216/140/14 - PB - 9781914424342 - Matt Lamination